Official Guide to the Wales Coast Path: Snowdonia & Ceredigion Coast

Shell Island, Gwynedd, from the air

@WalesCoastPath | @WalesCoastUK

www.walescoastpath.gov.uk | www.walescoastpath.co.uk

Official Guide to the

Wales Coast Path Snowdonia & Ceredigion Coast

Porthmadog to Cardigan

132 miles/ 213 kilometres of superb coastal walking

Vivienne Crow

Northern Eye
www.northerneyebooks.co.uk

Text: Vivienne Crow

Series editor: Tony Bowerman

Introductory section: Tony Bowerman

Photographs: Vivienne Crow, © Crown copyright (2021) Visit Wales, The National Trust, Janet Baxter Photography, Alamy, Shutterstock, Dreamstime, Carl Rogers

Design: Carl Rogers

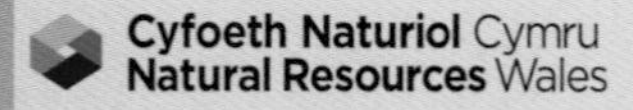

Northern Eye Books
ISBN 978-1-914589-03-4

A CIP catalogue record for this book is available from the British Library

www.northerneyebooks.co.uk
www.walescoastpath.co.uk

Twitter: @viviennecrow2
@Northerneyeboo
@WalesCoastUK

Important Advice: The route described in this book is undertaken at the reader's own risk. Walkers should take into account their level of fitness, wear suitable footwear and clothing, and carry food and water. It is also advisable to take the relevant OS maps with you in case you get lost and leave the area covered by our maps.

Whilst every care has been taken to ensure the accuracy of the route directions, the publishers cannot accept responsibility for errors or omissions, or for changes in the details given. Nor can the publisher and copyright owners accept responsibility for any consequences arising from the use of this book.

If you find any inaccuracies in either the text or maps, please write or email us at the addresses below. Thank you.

Acknowledgements: Warm thanks are due to everyone who helped make this book a reality. Thank you, in particular, to Natural Resources Wales' officer Quentin Grimley a for his friendly advice and support. Thanks to Claire Lillie at Arriva Trains Wales; Nigel Nicholas and Ann Eleri Jones at Ceredigion County Council; and Rhys Gwyn Roberts at Gwynedd Council. Thanks, too, to the many tourism officers, museum and library staff, Wales on View picture researchers, freelance photographers, and everyone else who has played their part. And, finally, thanks to Dave Quarrell for his passionate quote explaining why the Wales Coast Path is so special.

First published 2017

This rewalked and revised edition 2022

Northern Eye Books
Northern Eye Books, Tattenhall,
Cheshire CH3 9PX

Email: tony@northerneyebooks.com

For trade and sales enquiries, please call:
01928 723 744

Contents

Official Guides to the Wales Coast Path

The Official Guides to the Wales Coast Path are endorsed by **Natural Resources Wales**, the body responsible for coordinating the development of the route. The guides split the Path into seven main sections with a guide for each. Together, they cover the entire 870-mile Path from the outskirts of Chester in the north to Chepstow in the south.

For details of the full range of Official Guides to the Wales Coast Path, see: **www.walescoastpath.gov.uk/plan-your-trip/guidebooks/**

Wales Coast Path
Discover the shape of a nation

WALES IS THE LARGEST COUNTRY IN THE WORLD with a continuous path around its entire coast. The **Wales Coast Path** promises 870 miles/1,400 kilometres of unbroken coastal walking, from the outskirts of Chester in the north to Chepstow in the south. Along the way you'll experience the very best of Wales: stunning scenery, stirring history, Welsh culture, and wildlife in abundance. If you tackle only one big walk in your life, make it this one. It's unmissable.

Flint Castle, Flintshire

Bwa Gwyn sea arch, Anglesey

Atlantic grey seal

Caernarfon Castle, Gwynedd

Bardsey Island, Llyn Peninsula

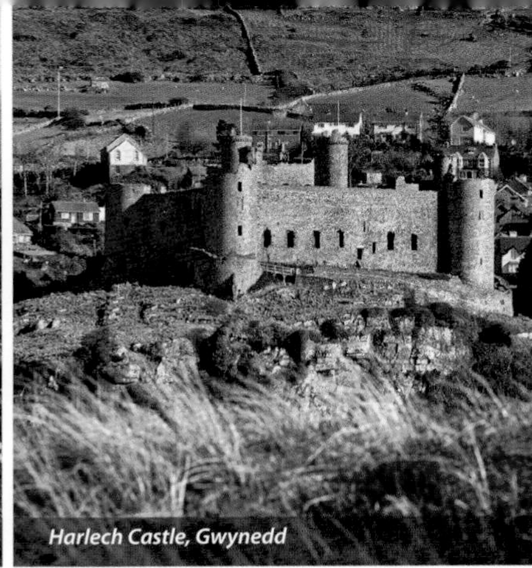

Harlech Castle, Gwynedd

St Govan's Chapel, Pembrokeshire

Bottlenose dolphin

Three Cliffs Bay, Gower

Chepstow Castle, Monmouthshire

Wales Coast Path

An 870-mile coastal adventure

WHEN THE **Wales Coast Path** OPENED IN MAY 2012, Wales became the largest country in the world with a continuous path around its entire coast. Walkers can now enjoy unparalleled coastal walking around the Welsh seaboard from top to bottom: from the outskirts of the ancient walled city of Chester, on the Dee estuary in the north, to the pretty market town of Chepstow, on the Severn Estuary, in the south.

The official, signposted and waymarked path covers roughly 870 miles/1400 kilometres and starts and finishes close to the ends of the historic 180 mile/285 kilometre Offa's Dyke National Trail. This means keen walkers can make a complete circumnavigation of Wales; a total distance of around 1,050 miles/1,690 kilometres. Ever keen for a new challenge, a few hardy walkers had already completed the full circuit within months of the Wales Coast Path's opening.

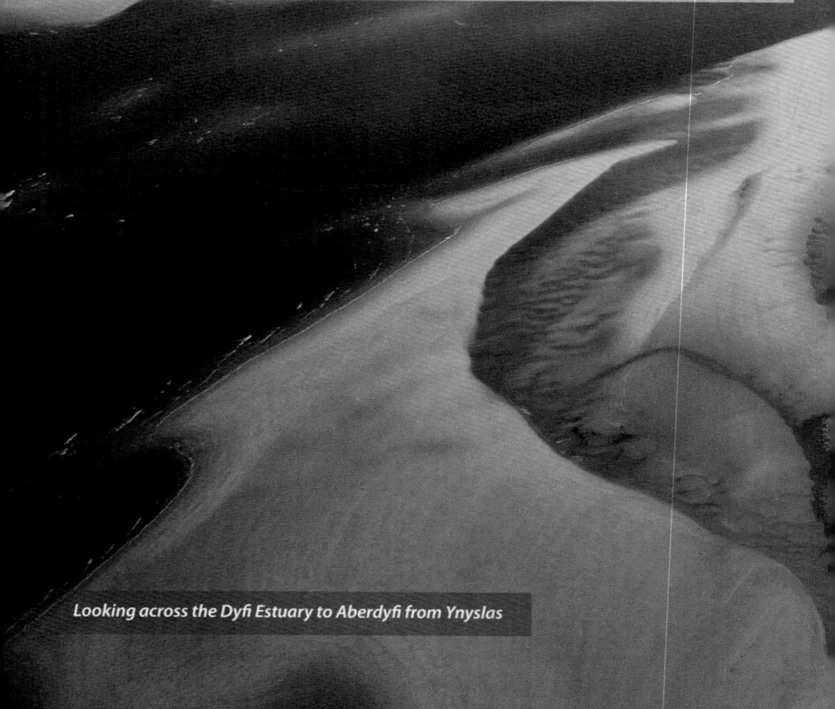

Looking across the Dyfi Estuary to Aberdyfi from Ynyslas

But whether you choose to walk the whole Path in one go, in occasional sections, or a few miles at a time, you're in for a real treat. There's something new around every corner, and you'll discover places that can only be reached on foot. Visually stunning and rich in both history and wildlife, the path promises ever-changing views, soaring cliffs and spacious beaches, sea caves and arches, wildflowers, seabirds, seals and dolphins, as well as castles, cromlechs, coves and coastal pubs. It's a genuinely special landscape.

This visual and ecological richness is recognised nationally and internationally. In fact, the Wales Coast Path runs through 1 Marine Nature Reserve, 1 Geopark, 2 National Parks, 3 Areas of Outstanding Natural Beauty, 3 World Heritage Sites, 7 official and unofficial nudist beaches, 11 National Nature Reserves, 14 Heritage Coasts, 17 Special Protection Areas, 21 Special Areas of Conservation, 23 Historic Landscapes, 42 Blue Flag beaches, and 111 marine Sites of Special Scientific Interest. Large stretches of coast are also managed and protected by Wildlife Trusts, the RSPB and the National Trust.

Long-distance walkers will enjoy the unbroken path, the solitude, the coast's constantly changing moods and the back-to-nature challenge. Holiday and weekend walkers can recharge their batteries, see something new, and regain a necessary sense of perspective. Families can potter, play and explore. And locals can walk the dog, jog, get fit and rediscover their home patch. Whatever your preferences, the Wales Coast Path promises something for everyone.

"Wales is beautiful, regardless of the weather ... and I would recommend the experience to anyone planning a similar trip!"

Zoe Wathen — the first woman to walk the whole Wales Coast Path

All or Part?

So, what's the best way to walk the Wales Coast Path? The 870 mile/1,400 kilometre route covers the whole of the Welsh seaboard and is the longest and probably the best of all Britain's long-distance challenges.

But of course, not everyone has the time, energy or inclination to walk it all at once. Instead, most people start with a short stretch, discover they love it, and come back for more.

Section by section

1 North Wales Coast

2 Isle of Anglesey

3 Llŷn Peninsula

4 Snowdonia & Ceredigion Coast

5 Pembrokeshire Coast Path

6 Carmarthen Bay & Gower

7 South Wales Coast

1. North Wales Coast

Chester to Bangor

80 miles/125 kilometres

7 Day Sections

Undulating coast. Vast Dee estuary, traditional seaside towns, limestone headland, and Conwy mountain

2. Isle of Anglesey

Circuit of island from Menai Bridge

125 miles/200 kilometres

12 Day Sections

Grand coastal scenery from tidal straits to bays, estuaries, dunes and cliffs. Area of Outstanding Natural Beauty

3. Llŷn Peninsula

Bangor to Porthmadog

110 miles/180 kilometres

9 Day Sections

Unspoilt peninsula with bays, coves and cliffs, tipped by Bardsey Island. Area of Outstanding Natural Beauty

4. Snowdonia & Ceredigion Coast

Porthmadog to Cardigan

132 miles/213 kilometres

11 Day Sections

Low-lying dunes and big estuaries followed by steeper, grassy sea cliffs with dramatic coves and bays

5. Pembrokeshire Coast Path

Cardigan to Tenby/Amroth

186 miles/300 kilometres

14 Day Sections

Varied, beautiful, popular. The Pembrokeshire Coastal Path is a National Trail and coastal National Park

6. Carmarthen Bay & Gower

Tenby to Swansea

130 miles/208 kilometres

12 Day Sections

Long sandy beaches, tidal estuaries, dramatic rocky coast. Area of Outstanding Natural Beauty

7. South Wales Coast

Swansea to Chepstow

115 miles/185 kilometres

9 Day Sections

Traditional beach resorts, seafaring and industrial landscapes. Heritage Coast, National Nature Reserves

Sense of space: *Walkers exploring the dunes at Gronant, North Wales*

Wales: Top to bottom

Walking the whole 870 miles/1,400 kilometres of the Wales Coast Path in one go is an increasingly popular challenge. Some people have even run all the way. By a curious coincidence, the overall distance is almost exactly the same as Britain's famous top-to-bottom route, from John o' Groats to Land's End — a very long way.

The Wales Coast Path will take you from the outskirts of Chester down the broad Dee estuary, along the North Wales coast with its traditional seaside resorts and impressive limestone headlands at Little and Great Orme, past Conwy Castle, over Conwy Mountain and on along the wooded Menai Straits. The Path then loops around the rugged, offshore Isle of Anglesey, or Ynys Môn, passes the walled town of Caernarfon and its castle before heading around the remote Llŷn Peninsula with Bardsey Island balanced at its tip. From Criccieth and Porthmadog the Path pushes south past Harlech castle — kissing the western rim of the Snowdonia National Park — and on down the majestic sweep of Cardigan Bay with its beautiful, open estuaries. It then rounds Pembrokeshire — Britain's only coastal National Park — with its

sparkling bays and lofty cliffs. Striding through Carmarthenshire and crossing the wide Towy and Tâf estuaries, the Path curves around the lovely Gower Peninsula into Swansea Bay. Beyond the striking Glamorgan Heritage Coast, the Path runs along the Cardiff Bay waterfront to Cardiff, the lively capital of Wales. From there, it's only a short stretch alongside the broad Severn estuary to the pretty market town of Chepstow on the Welsh-English border and the southern end of the Wales Coast Path.

Only the fittest, most determined walkers can hope to complete the entire Path in 6-7 weeks, averaging 20 or so miles a day.

At a more leisurely pace — allowing time to soak up the atmosphere and enjoy the views, and with regular pauses to watch the wildlife, swim, enjoy a quiet drink or visit some of the fascinating places along the way — you should allow around 3 months for the whole trip.

Remember, though, the Wales Coast Path is a challenging route with plenty of rough ground, narrow paths and ups-and-downs (an overall total ascent and descent of 95,800 feet/ 29,200 metres). There are tempting detours and places to see along the way, too. So it's perhaps best to plan slightly shorter and more realistic daily distances than you might ordinarily cover.

You should also allow extra time for the unexpected, to rest or to hole up in bad weather. As a rule of thumb, it's better to be ahead of schedule, with time to enjoy the experience, rather than always having to push ahead to reach the next overnight stop.

The Official Guidebooks in this series break the path down into seven main sections (see the map on page 10), each of which is then sub-divided into carefully-planned 'Day Sections' — usually averaging around 10-15 miles each. These typically start and finish either in, or near easy-to-reach towns, villages or settlements, many of them on bus routes, and with shops, pubs, restaurants, cafés and places to stay nearby.

No matter how long it takes, walking the whole of the Wales Coast Path is a real achievement. For most of us, it would be the walk of a lifetime.

Walking around Wales a bit at a time

Yet, understandably, most people don't want to walk the whole path in one go. Instead, they prefer to do it bit by bit, often over several years: during annual and bank holidays, over long weekends, or as the whim takes them. Done in this leisurely fashion, the walk becomes a project to ponder, plan, and take pleasure in.

A popular way to enjoy the path is to book a short holiday close to a section of the path, and do a series of day walks along the surrounding coast, returning to your base each night.

Evening storm light highlights the old lighthouse at Llandwyn Island, Anglesey

Medieval might: *Edward I's distinctive castle at Caernarfon*

Some people like to catch a train (especially along the North Wales Coast), bus or taxi to the start of their day's walk and then walk back (see the information at the start of each day section).

Another approach is to drive to the end of your planned section and then get a pre-booked local taxi to take you back to the start; this costs only a few pounds and lets you walk in one direction at your own pace.

If you're planning to walk a section over several days before returning to your starting point by bus or train, call Traveline on 0870 6082608 or visit **www.traveline-cymru.org.uk** for help with timetables and itineraries.

Best time to go?

Britain's main walking season runs from Easter to the end of September. Although the Wales Coast Path is delightful throughout the year, the best walking weather tends to be in late spring as well as early and late summer.

Although the Easter holiday is busy, spring is otherwise a quiet time of year. The days are lengthening and the weather getting steadily warmer. Migrant birds and basking sharks are returning to Wales from farther south. The weather is also likely to be dry.

Early summer is ideal for walking. May and June enjoy the greatest number

Pub on the beach: *The Ty Coch at Porth Dinllaen is a popular summer watering hole*

of sunshine hours per day (the average for May is 225 hours, and for June 210 hours) and the lowest rainfall of the year (average for May is 50mm, June is 51mm). You'll also have the accompaniment of a spectacular array of spring flowers and the chance to see breeding sea birds at their best.

High summer is the busiest season, particularly during the school holidays in July and August. Both the beaches and the Coast Path are likely to be packed in places. Finding somewhere to stay at short notice can be tricky, too — so it's best to book well in advance. However, the long sunny days are certainly attractive, and you can often walk in shorts and a T-shirt.

By September most visitors have returned home, and you'll have the Coast Path largely to yourself. The weather remains good and the sea is still warm enough for swimming. Sunny days often stretch into September, with the first of the winter storms arriving in late September and October. Autumn also means the coastal trees and bracken are slowly turning from green to red, orange and gold.

Winter brings shorter, colder days with less sunlight and other disadvantages: unpredictable weather, stormy seas, high winds and even gales

along with closed cafés and accommodation. But for experienced walkers, the cooler days can bring peace and solitude and a heightened sense of adventure.

Welsh weather

Like the rest of Britain, Wales is warmed by the Gulf Stream's ocean current and enjoys a temperate climate. This is particularly true of the country's west coast. Because Wales lies in the west of Britain, the weather is generally mild but damp. Low pressure fronts typically come in off the Irish Sea from the west and southwest, hitting the coast first and then moving inland to the east. This means rain and wet weather can occur at any time of year, so you should always take good waterproofs and spare clothes with you.

For more weather or a five-day forecast, visit **www.metoffice.com** or **www.bbc.co.uk/weather**. Several premium-rate national 'Weatherlines' give up-to-date forecasts, and the Snowdonia and Pembrokeshire National Parks websites provide local information, too.

Which direction?

The Official Guide books give directions from north to south, starting in Chester and ending in Chepstow. This means walkers will enjoy the sun on their faces for much of the way. Most luggage transfer services also run in this direction. Nonetheless, the path can be tackled in either direction. It's just easier to go with the flow.

Which section?

Choosing which part of the Wales Coast Path to walk depends in part on where you live, how long you've got, and the kind of scenery you prefer.

Sections vary considerably. Arry Beresford-Webb, the first person to run the entire Path in 2012 said, 'I was stunned by the diversity of the Path. Each section felt like I was going through a different country.'

Some stretches are fairly wild, while others are more developed. Parts of the Isle of Anglesey, Llŷn Peninsula, Cardigan Bay and Pembrokeshire are often remote and away from large settlements. Other stretches, such as North Wales or the South Wales coast around Swansea, Cardiff and Newport are busier, and often close to popular seaside towns or industry.

The terrain varies too. Much of the North Wales coast is low-lying but punctuated with occasional headlands; as are much of Cardigan Bay, Carmarthen Bay and parts of the Glamorgan Heritage Coast.

Portmeirion is a fantastic Italianate village on the Afon Dwyryd

In contrast, the Isle of Anglesey, Llŷn Peninsula, Pembrokeshire and Gower are often rocky with high sea cliffs, dramatic headlands, offshore islands and intimate coves.

Self sufficient or supported?

The other key decision for walkers is whether to arrange everything yourself or let experts do it for you. For many people, devising their own itinerary and working out how to travel and where to stay is part of the fun. Others prefer to let one of the specialist walking holiday companies create the itinerary, book accommodation, arrange luggage transfers, meals and side trips. The main companies are listed at the back of the book.

Accommodation

There are plenty of places to stay within easy reach of the Wales Coast Path all around Wales. Most walkers either camp or stay in bed and breakfast accommodation; usually a mix of the two. There are plenty of hostels and bunkhouses along the way but, unfortunately, they are too unevenly spaced to provide accommodation every night.

Accommodation may be fully booked during peak holiday seasons, so it's advisable to book well ahead. Local Tourist Information Centres (TICs) will often know all the local accommodation providers, know who has vacancies, and can help with booking. For late, or emergency on-the-spot bookings, it's also worth contacting the TICs listed at the start of each day section.

Backpacking

Backpacking adds an extra dimension to the walking experience: being outdoors for days at a time, watching the sunrise and sunset, gazing at the stars overhead without artificial light getting in the way. But don't underestimate how much a heavy pack can slow you down. The secret is to travel as light as possible; the lightest tent or bivvi bag, a lightweight sleeping bag and waterproofs, and a single change of clothes.

There are plenty of official campsites along the busier sections of the Wales Coast Path. However, many are on small farms and may not advertise. Elsewhere campsites are often few and far between, and may need searching for. During peak season some may also be full, so it's advisable to book ahead. But remember, most sites are closed during the winter (typically from November to Easter, and often longer).

Unofficial 'wild camping' is a grey area. There is no legal right in England or Wales to 'wild camp' anywhere, including alongside the path. Every scrap of

Sand castle: *Harlech Castle overlooks the broad coastal dunes*

land in Britain belongs to someone, and many landowners frown on campers. So it makes sense to ask before pitching.

Unofficially, however, overnight camping is usually tolerated, so long as you pitch a small tent unobtrusively in the evening, and pack up and leave early the next morning, without leaving a trace.

Alternatively, there are popular luggage transfer services on the more established stretches of the Path. For a small fee, they wiil pick up your rucksack and other bags and transport them to the end of your day's walk. A list of luggage transfer companies appears at the back of the book.

Clothes, boots and backpack

For those new to long-distance walking, it's worth emphasising the benefits of comfortable walking boots and suitable clothing. Walking continuously, day after day, puts extra pressures on your feet. Be prepared for changes in the weather, too. Carry waterproofs and remember that several thin layers allow you to adjust your clothing as conditions change.

Checking the weather forecast before you set off each day will help you decide what to wear. If you're in the car, it's worth taking a selection of clothing for different conditions, and deciding what to wear and carry immediately before you start.

Onshore breezes can mask the strength of the sun. To avoid sunburn, or even sunstroke, remember to slap on some sunscreen and wear a hat.

Other things to take, depending on weight, include: maps, water bottle, lightweight walking poles, basic First Aid including plasters and antiseptic cream, penknife, head torch and spare batteries, chocolate, sweets or energy bars, toilet paper, a small camera, binoculars, mobile phone, and a pen and notebook. Don't forget some spare cash too; most places accept cards but finding a Cashpoint or somewhere that offers 'Cash Back' near the Path can be tricky.

Mwnt church perches above the rocky Ceredigion coast

Summer daze: *The iconic Three Cliffs Bay, Gower*

Food and drink

Although the official guidebooks try to start and end each day at places with amenities, some sections are nonetheless remote and may have few places to buy food or drink. This may be the case for several days in a row. So it makes sense to plan ahead and carry enough supplies with you.

Conversely, other sections are well supplied with shops, pubs, cafés, restaurants and takeaways, and these are indicated at the start of each Day Section.

Maps

The maps in this book are based on the Ordnance Survey Landranger 1:50,000 series, with the line of the Wales Coast Path highlighted in orange. The numbers on the maps correspond to those in the route description for each Day Section.

The best maps for walking are the larger scale, orange-covered Ordnance Survey Explorer 1:25,000 scale maps, which show additional features such as Access Land, field boundaries, springs and wells. Both scales of OS maps now have the official route of the Wales Coast Path marked on them: as a line composed of a series of red diamonds on the 1:50,000 Landranger maps, and green diamonds on the 1:25,000 Explorer maps.

The relevant maps for each Day Section are listed at the beginning of each chapter. The grid references given in this book for the start and finish of each Day Section are from the Ordnance Survey maps.

Route finding

For the most part, the Wales Coast Path follows a single official route. In a few places, there are both official and unofficial alternative routes. Otherwise, the path hugs the coast as far is practically and legally possible, occasionally diverting inland around private estates, nature reserves, natural obstacles, estuaries, gunnery ranges and so on. The definitive route, and any occasional changes are notified on the official Wales Coast Path website.

The path uses a mixture of public rights of way: footpaths, bridleways and byways as well as lanes, open access land, beaches and some permissive paths. On most sections, the route is well-used and clear. In remote or under-used areas, however, walkers will need to pay closer attention to the maps and directions in this book.

Nesting seabirds on Elegug Stacks, Pembrokeshire

Way to go: *Distinctive signs and waymarkers with the Wales Coast Path symbol mark the route*

Fingerposts and waymarkers

The Wales Coast Path is clearly signed and waymarked with its own distinctive logo: a white dragon-tailed seashell on a blue background surrounded by a yellow circlet bearing the words *'Llwybr Arfordir Cymru – Wales Coast Path'*. Look for the wood or metal fingerposts at main access points, in towns, on roadsides and lanes, and at key junctions.

Official route waymarkers

Official alternative route waymarker

Elsewhere the route is clearly waymarked with plastic roundels fixed to stiles, gateposts, fences and walls. In many places the Wales Coast Path waymarkers sit alongside others for already established routes — such as the Isle of Anglesey Coastal Path or the Pembrokeshire Coast Path National Trail. In some areas these local waymarkers are still more in evidence than the official Wales Coast Path ones; and on some stretches, waymarking remains patchy.

Alternative routes

Two sorts of alternative route are described in the guides. The first are the **official alternative routes** that avoid remote or challenging sections; and more attractive routes that, for example, provide better views or get farther away from motor traffic.

The second are our own **unofficial alternative routes**. Many of these are beach routes below the high water mark that by their nature are not permanently available, and so do not qualify as part of the 'official route'. Others are alternative high level routes or simply 'better' or more attractive, in our opinion. Both the **official** and **unofficial alternative routes** are shown on the maps in this book as a broken orange highlight.

Detours

The directions also describe **detours** to places of interest that we think you won't want to miss. These are usually short, off the main Path, there-and-back routes, typically of no more than a kilometre or so in each direction. Suggested detours can take you to anything from a special pub, castle or church to a stunning view or waterfall. If you've got the time, they bring an extra dimension to the walk. Detours are shown as a blue broken highlight.

Temporary diversions

There may be occasional or seasonal temporary inland diversions. The reasons for them vary from land management and public safety, such as forestry work, cliff falls, landslips and floods, to wildlife conservation — protecting seal breeding sites, bird roosts and nesting sites, and so on. Details of the latest permanent and temporary diversions can be found on the official Wales Coast Path website under 'Route Changes'. See **www.walescoastpath.gov.uk.**

Tides and tide tables

As much as five percent of the Wales Coast Path runs along the foreshore, between mean high and low water. These sections are naturally affected by the tide. On the whole, the official Wales Coast Path avoids beaches and estuaries. However, beaches often provide time-honoured, direct and pleasant walking routes and are usually safely accessible, except for around 1½ hours either side of high tide. If the tide is in, or you're in any doubt, take the inland route instead.

Occasional streams and tidal creeks may also be crossed at low tide but be impassable at high water. So it is a good idea to carry tide tables with you and consult them before you set out each day. They are widely available for around £1 from coastal TICs, shops and newsagents.

Ancient layers: *Limestone cliffs at Nash Point on the Glamorgan Heritage Coast, South Wales*

Several websites also give accurate tidal predictions for locations around the UK, including downloadable five day predictions. Useful websites include: **www.bbc.co.uk/weather/coast_and_sea/tide_tables** and **www.easytide.ukho.gov.uk**.

Safety advice

If you're new to long-distance walking, or in one of the remoter areas, please remember:

- Wear walking boots and warm, waterproof clothing.
- Take food and drink.
- Mobile signals are patchy along much of the Path; let someone know where you are heading and when you expect to arrive.
- If you decide to walk along a beach, always check tide tables.
- Stay on the path and away from cliff edges.
- Take extra care in windy and/or wet conditions.
- Always supervise children and dogs.
- Follow local signs and diversions.

Emergencies

In an emergency, call 999 or 112 and ask for the service you require: Ambulance, Police, Fire or Coastguard.

Tell them your location as accurately as possible (give an OS grid reference, if possible; and look for named landmarks), how many people are in your party, and the nature of the problem.

Remember, though, that mobile signals may be poor or absent in some areas. Some coastal car parks and main beach access points have emergency telephones. Coastal pubs and shops may also have phones you can ask to use in an emergency.

Who manages the Path?

The Wales Coast Path is co-ordinated at a national level by Natural Resources Wales and managed on the ground by the sixteen local authorities and two National Parks through which it passes.

Funding has come from the Welsh Government, the European Regional Development Fund and the local authorities themselves.

For more details, see: **www.naturalresourceswales.gov.uk.**

Best of the **Snowdonia & Ceredigion** Coast

The **Snowdonia & Ceredigion coast** offers a tremendous variety of landscape to those who walk its entire 213km: from high, airy cliff-tops to secluded coves; from estuarine salt marshes to beaches backed by tremendous dune systems that stretch on for miles. And with that diversity comes a huge range of wildlife, including seabirds, choughs, dolphins and rare wildflowers. The history too changes with every twist and turn of this fascinating route: visitors should always be prepared for the unexpected in a region that contains the ruins of once mighty castles and has links with characters as disparate as King Arthur and members of the rock band Led Zeppelin.

Portmeirion

Harlech Castle

Barmouth bridge

Aberdyfi

Machynlleth

Ynyslas National Nature Reserve

Aberystwyth

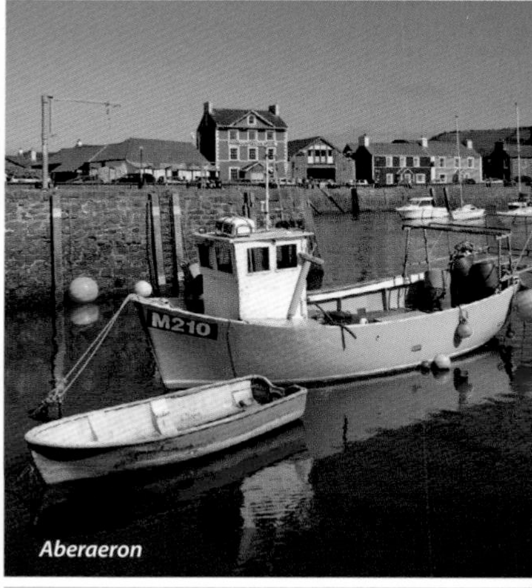

Aberaeron

New Quay

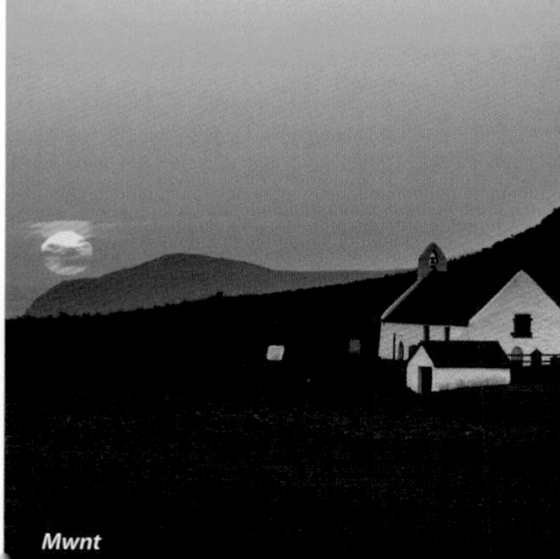
Mwnt

"Walking is a man's best medicine."

Hippocrates, *Greek physician, circa 400 BC*

Snowdonia & Ceredigion Coast

Part of the **Wales Coast Path**

The **Snowdonia** & **Ceredigion Coast** probably offers a more diverse walking experience than any other section of the Wales Coast Path. The stretch covered in this book — from Porthmadog in the north to Cardigan in the south — largely covers two contrasting Welsh counties.

The first 97 kilometres pass through Gwynedd, along the western edge of the Snowdonia National Park. Here, just before the rivers that rise in the highest of the Welsh mountains reach the sea, they fan out to form broad estuaries that provide rich pickings for waders and other birdlife. The estuaries of the Dwyryd, the Mawddach and the Dyfi are the largest of these. Between them are some very large dune systems, including Morfa Harlech and Morfa Dyffryn — home to rare wildlife. Here, walkers are able to stride out along seemingly endless beaches, often with spectacular views inland to the mountains of Snowdonia or across the bay to the peaks of the Llŷn peninsula.

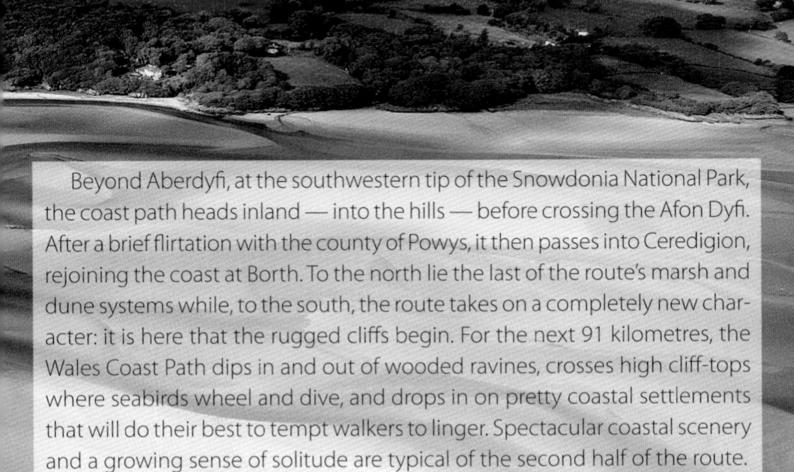

Beyond Aberdyfi, at the southwestern tip of the Snowdonia National Park, the coast path heads inland — into the hills — before crossing the Afon Dyfi. After a brief flirtation with the county of Powys, it then passes into Ceredigion, rejoining the coast at Borth. To the north lie the last of the route's marsh and dune systems while, to the south, the route takes on a completely new character: it is here that the rugged cliffs begin. For the next 91 kilometres, the Wales Coast Path dips in and out of wooded ravines, crosses high cliff-tops where seabirds wheel and dive, and drops in on pretty coastal settlements that will do their best to tempt walkers to linger. Spectacular coastal scenery and a growing sense of solitude are typical of the second half of the route.

In total, the 213 kilometres should take about 11 days to walk. And, with no two days the same, it promises to be a varied and fascinating experience.

An aerial view of Portmeirion village on the Dwyryd Estuary

Walking the Snowdonia & Ceredigion Coast

The Snowdonia & Ceredigion Coast section of the Wales Coast Path runs for 132 miles / 213 kilometres between Porthmadog in Gwynedd in the north and the town of Cardigan close to the Pembrokeshire border in the south. This guide splits the route into 11 convenient Day Sections, each of about 6-18 miles / 10-29 kilometres. (Day Sections six and seven also provide route descriptions for the Ceredigion Coast Path which, for a few kilometres north of Borth, doesn't coincide with the Wales Coast Path.)

All these sections start and finish in towns or villages with facilities for eating, sleeping and buying provisions. However, some of the smaller villages have limited accommodation options, so you are advised to book early. There are good public transport links all along the route should you need to catch a bus or train at the end of the day to reach a bed for the night. All the Day Sections are shown on the chart below.

Day Section	Distance	Start	Finish
Day Section 1 Porthmadog to Harlech	11 miles 19 km	Porthmadog SH 570 384	Harlech SH 580 313
Day Section 2 Harlech to Barmouth	17 miles 27 km	Harlech SH 580 313	Barmouth SH 615 154
Day Section 3 Barmouth to Llwyngwril	8 miles 14 km	Barmouth SH 615 154	Llwyngwril SH 591 093
Day Section 4 Llwyngwril to Aberdyfi	12 miles 19 km	Llwyngwril SH 591 093	Aberdyfi SH 614 959
Day Section 5 Aberdyfi to Machynlleth	12 miles 19 km	Aberdifi SH 614 959	Machynlleth SH 745 007
Day Section 6 Machynlleth to Borth	18 miles 29 km	Machynlleth SH 745 007	Borth SN 608 889
Ceredigion Coast Path			
Day Section 7 Ynyslas to Aberystwyth	9 miles 15 km	Ynys Las SN 609 941	Aberystwyth SN 581 818
Day Section 8 Aberystwyth to Llanon	13 miles 21 km	Aberystwyth SN 581 818	Llanon SN 507 667

Day Section	Distance	Start	Finish
Day Section 9 Llanon to New Quay	11 miles 18 km	Llanon SN 507 667	New Quay SN 389 600
Day Section 10 New Quay to Aberporth	13 miles 21 km	New Quay SN 389 600	Aberporth SN 258 515
Day Section 11 Aberporth to Cardigan	13 miles 21 km	Aberporth SN 258 515	Cardigan SN 177 458

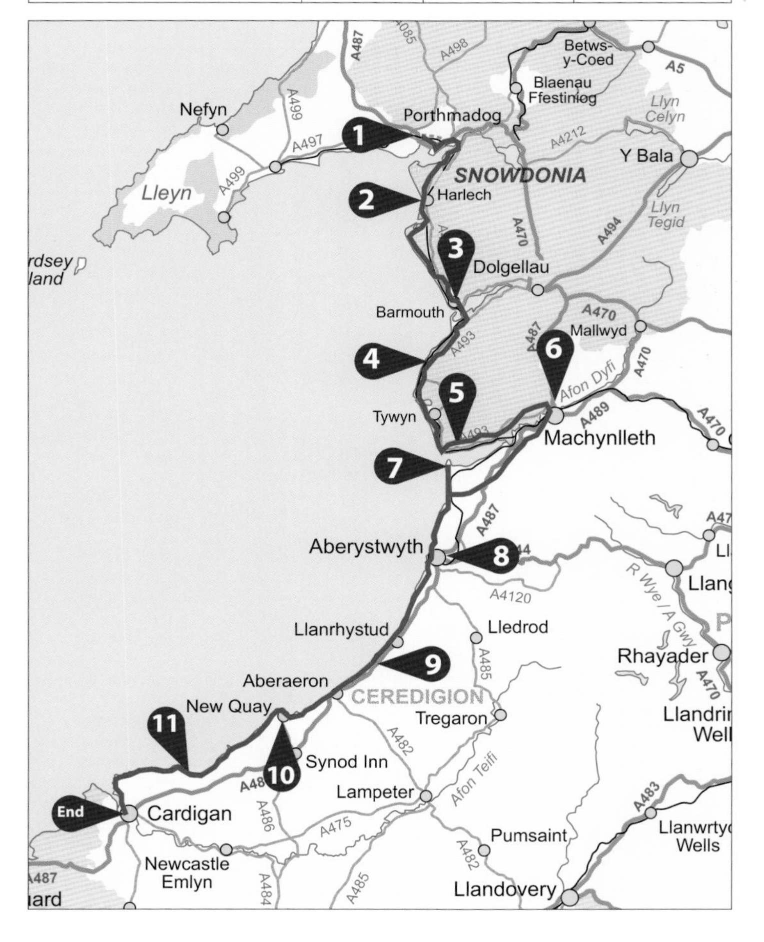

Distance chart for key locations along the path

Miles / Kilometres

	Porthmadog	Penrhyndeudraeth	Harlech	Llanbedr	Tal-y-Bont	Barmouth	Fairbourne	Llwyngwril	Tywyn	Aberdyfi	Penal	Machynlleth	Furnace	Tre'r ddôl	Borth	Aberystwyth	Llanrhystud	Llanon	Aberaeron	New Quay	Llangranog	Aberporth	Mwnt	Cardigan
Porthmadog		4	12	16	23	28	31	37	44	49	56	61	68	71	75	82	92	94	99	105	114	119	124	131
Penrhyndeudraeth	7		8	12	19	24	27	33	40	45	52	57	64	67	71	78	88	90	95	101	109	115	120	127
Harlech	19	12		5	12	16	20	25	33	37	44	49	57	59	64	70	80	82	87	94	102	107	112	119
Llanbedr	26	20	7		7	12	15	20	28	32	40	44	52	55	59	65	75	77	83	89	97	102	108	115
Tal-y-Bont	38	31	19	12		5	8	13	21	25	33	37	45	47	52	58	68	70	76	82	90	95	100	108
Barmouth	45	38	26	19	7		3	9	16	21	28	33	40	43	47	54	64	66	71	77	86	91	96	103
Fairbourne	50	43	31	24	12	5		6	13	17	25	30	37	40	44	51	61	63	68	74	82	88	93	100
Llwyngwril	59	52	40	33	21	14	9		8	12	19	24	32	34	39	45	55	57	62	69	77	82	87	94
Tywyn	71	65	53	45	34	26	21	12		4	12	16	24	27	31	37	47	49	55	61	69	74	80	87
Aberdyfi	78	72	60	52	41	33	28	19	7		7	12	20	22	27	33	43	45	50	57	65	70	75	82
Penal	90	83	71	64	52	45	40	31	19	12		5	12	15	19	26	36	38	43	49	58	63	68	75
Machynlleth	98	91	79	72	60	53	48	39	26	19	8		8	10	15	21	31	33	38	45	53	58	63	70
Furnace	110	103	91	84	72	65	60	51	38	32	20	12		3	7	13	23	26	31	37	45	51	56	63
Tre'r ddôl	114	107	95	88	76	69	64	55	43	36	24	16	4		4	11	21	23	28	34	43	48	53	60
Borth	121	115	103	95	84	76	71	62	50	43	31	24	11	4		6	16	18	24	30	38	43	49	56
Aberystwyth	131	125	113	105	94	86	81	72	60	53	41	34	22	17	10		10	12	17	24	32	37	42	49
Llanrhystud	147	141	129	121	110	103	97	89	76	69	58	50	38	34	26	16		2	7	14	22	27	32	39
Llanon	151	144	132	125	113	106	101	92	79	73	61	53	41	37	30	19	3		5	11	20	25	30	37
Aberaeron	159	153	141	133	122	114	109	100	88	81	69	62	50	45	38	28	12	8		6	15	20	25	32
New Quay	169	163	151	143	132	124	119	110	98	91	79	72	60	55	48	38	22	18	10		8	14	19	26
Llangranog	183	176	164	157	145	138	133	124	111	105	93	85	73	69	62	51	35	32	24	14		5	10	17
Aberporth	191	184	172	165	153	146	141	132	120	113	101	93	81	77	70	60	44	40	32	22	8		5	12
Mwnt	199	193	181	173	162	154	149	140	128	121	109	102	90	85	78	68	52	49	40	30	17	8		7
Cardigan	211	204	192	185	173	166	161	152	139	133	121	113	101	97	90	79	63	60	52	42	28	20	11	

Distances are approximate to the nearest mile/kilometre

Day Sections

1: Porthmadog to Harlech

Distance: 11 miles/19 kilometres

Terrain: Woodland and wildlife-rich estuaries along the western edge of the Snowdonia National Park.

Points of interest: Ffestiniog and Welsh Highland Railways; Portmeirion, Italianate village; Afon Dwyryd estuary, a winter feeding ground for wildfowl; former site of Europe's largest explosives works .

Note: A good range of facilities in Porthmadog and Harlech. Like many stretches of the path through Gwynedd, this section passes several stations on the Cambrian Coast railway line, providing points at which the day could be cut short.

Portmeirion Italianate village, Gwynedd

2: Harlech to Barmouth

Distance: 17 miles/27 kilometres

Terrain: Wildlife-rich wetlands and two long beaches backed by immense dune systems; some field paths and riverside trails; long section beside main road at the end of the day.

Points of interest: Harlech Castle; literary connections; St Tanwg's Church; Pensarn Harbour; wildlife, dunes and beaches at Morfa Harlech and Morfa Dyffryn.

Note: A good range of facilities in both Harlech and Barmouth. There are other places to stay and to eat all along this section of the route. As on the previous day, stations along the Cambrian Coast railway line are never far away.

3: Barmouth to Llwyngwril

Distance: 8 miles/ 14 kilometres

Terrain: Salt marsh and section along sea wall; climb through a fascinating disused slate quarry; quiet hill road; grassy paths and farm tracks .

Points of interest: Barmouth harbour and historic buildings; Barmouth Bridge, the longest bridge in Wales; Fairbourne Steam Railway; the Blue Lake, flooded quarry pit; prehistoric settlements and standing stones.

Note: Barmouth has a wide range of facilities, but choice is more limited in Llwyngwril. As on previous days, the Cambrian Coast railway line opens up the options in terms of places to stay .

Harlech Castle

Idyllic inlet: *Barmouth and its famous bridge dominate the mouth of the Mawddach estuary*

4: Llwyngwril to Aberdyfi

Distance: 12 miles/ 19 kilometres

Terrain: Worn trackways and trails across ancient, farmed landscape; quiet country lanes; sea wall through Tywyn; long, sandy beach.

Points of interest: Iron Age fort; impressive bowspring bridge; Broad Water, a Site of Special Scientific Interest; Talyllyn Railway; the Cadfan Stone, the earliest known example of written Welsh.

Note: Facilities are limited in Llwyngwril, but Tywyn and Aberdyfi are larger settlements. The Cambrian Coast railway line, with its frequent stations, continues to run more or less parallel with the coast path.

5: Aberdyfi to Machynlleth

Distance: 12 miles/ 19 kilometres

Terrain: Hill track; farm paths; forest tracks; road walking.

Points of interest: Extensive views from Panorama Walk; medieval hall house; sites associated with King Arthur, Owain Glyndŵr and Led Zeppelin.

Note: Aberdyfi isn't a huge settlement, but it does have accommodation, several places to eat, some small shops and public toilets. Machynlleth is the

Traditional resort: *Aberystwyth's seafront hotels reflected in the sea at night*

largest town since Porthmadog and, as such, has a wide range of facilities. Between the two, the only village of note is Pennal — with pub, small shop and public toilets. Railway stations at Aberdyfi, Penhelig and Machynlleth only.

6: Machynlleth to Borth

Distance: 15 miles/ 24 kilometres (18 miles / 29 kilometres)

Terrain: Farm and woodland paths; open hillside; road walking, mostly quiet lanes; wildlife-rich marshland. Long section of beach/road for those continuing on the Ceredigion Coast Path to Ynyslas.

Points of interest: Museum and medieval townhouse; well-preserved iron furnace; Cors Fochno National Nature Reserve; pet graveyard; submerged forest.

Note: There are good facilities at either end of this section as well as B&Bs, pub, café and community shop at Tre'r-ddôl. Rail links are poorer now, but the stretch between Machynlleth and Tre'r-ddôl is never far from the A487, so it is easy to drop down to the main road to find accommodation or catch a bus.

7: Borth (or Ynyslas) to Aberystwyth

Distance: 6 miles / 10 kilometres, (or 9 miles/15 kilometres)

Terrain: Mostly cliff-top walking, although there's a long section of beach/road for those walking all of the Ceredigion Coast Path.

Points of interest: Narrow-gauge steam railway; interesting geological features; camera obscura on Constitution Hill; funicular cliff railway; museum.

Note: Again, there are good facilities at either end of this section, particularly in Aberystwyth, the largest town between Porthmadog and Cardigan. There are also holiday parks, a campsite, café and fast food en route. Borth and Aberystwyth are linked by rail and bus.

8: Aberystwyth to Llanon

Distance: 13 miles/ 21 kilometres

Terrain: Cliff-top paths; heathland; gently rolling farmland; short section on roads.

Points of interest: Ruins of Aberystwyth Castle; prehistoric remains at Pen Dinas; cliff-face hanging oak woodland; nesting seabirds in summer; industrial-scale limekilns.

Safe harbour: *New Quay is a popular seaside resort on the Ceredigion coast*

Note: Few facilities en route, apart from at Llanrhystud, where there are shops, accommodation and a pub. Llanon, at day's end, has some facilities, but the choice is limited. Aberystwyth is the last place with rail links, but there are buses between the town and Llanrhystud/Llanon.

9: Llanon to New Quay

Distance: 11 miles/ 18 kilometres

Terrain: Field paths; cliffs; woodland; pavements through Aberaeron; beach.

Points of interest: Ancient strip field system; medieval fish traps; colourful harbour town of Aberaeron; long, sandy beaches.

Note: Llanon has limited facilities. There is more choice in Aberaeron and New Quay. All three settlements are on bus routes.

10: New Quay to Aberporth

Distance: 13 miles / 21km

Terrain: High, windswept cliffs and secluded coves; small coastal villages; inland alternative mostly involves roads, woodland and field paths.

Points of interest: Links with Dylan Thomas; Marine Wildlife Centre; seabird colonies; rare butterflies; Iron Age forts; pretty villages; impressive geological features.

Note: New Quay and Aberporth, both of which are on bus routes, offer a decent range of accommodation and places to eat, although the latter has little in the way of shops. There are facilities at several villages en-route.

11: Aberporth to Cardigan

Distance: 13 miles / 21km

Terrain: Cliff-top paths and steep-sided cwms; minor roads and farmland along the eastern shore of the Teifi estuary.

Points of interest: Attractive coastal scenery; medieval chapel of ease for sailors; sheltered beach at Mwnt; colourful market town of Cardigan.

Note: Cardigan has a greater range of facilities than Aberporth, but there is little en route other than the limited facilities at Mwnt and Gwbert.

The old bridge across Afon Teifi at Cardigan

Limited for time? — The **Snowdonia & Ceredigion Coast** in a nutshell

If you have limited time to explore the Snowdonia and Ceredigion Coast section of the Wales Coast Path — perhaps only a weekend, or even just one day — you might want to consider visiting these unmissable sections.

Using local buses, enjoy an atmospheric one-day walk from the vibrant town of Aberystwyth to Llanrhystud — through a coastal landscape with a lonely, isolated feel to it. It's a day of cliff-top walking interspersed with gently rolling farmland and bracken-covered slopes just back from the precipice. In places, twenty-first century walkers follow ancient routeways where the incessant passage of travellers has, over the ages, worn a groove into otherwise smooth, grassy hillsides.

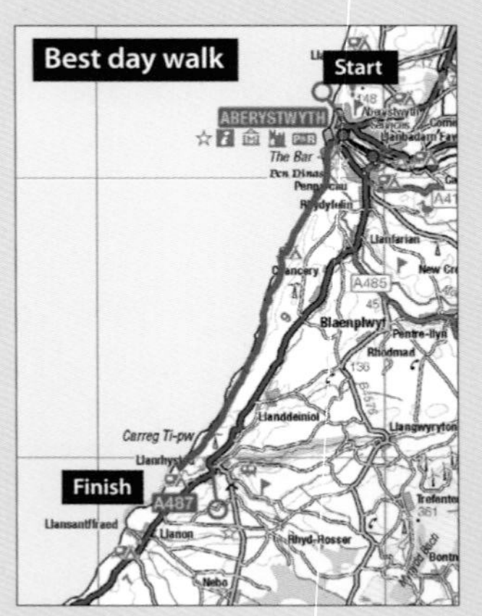

Alternatively, for a superb two-day walk along even more dramatic cliffs, use local buses to start your walk at New Quay and continue to Cardigan, breaking your walk at Aberporth. Be prepared for two days of windswept, roller-coaster walking through some of the most spectacular coastal scenery on this stretch of the Wales Coast Path. Pretty villages along the way provide opportunities for leisurely refreshment stops.

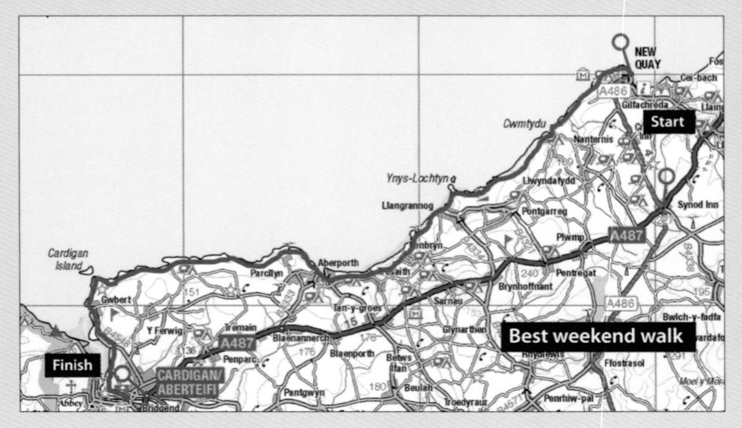

Best day walk

A gentle landscape of rolling cliffs and heathland

Aberystwyth to Llanrhystud: 10½ miles /17 kilometres

The walk follows the same route as Day Section 8, from Aberystwyth as far as point 9 in the walk description. From here, walk northeast along the A487 — into the village of Llanrhystud to catch the bus back to Aberystwyth.

Llanrhystud coast

Best weekend walk

High, dramatic cliffs and secluded coves

New Quay to Cardigan: 26 miles/42 kilometres

Day One: 13 miles / 21km: Day Section 10, starting in New Quay and then following the coast path southwest through the tiny settlements of Cwmtydu and Llangrannog, ending at Aberporth.

Day Two: 13 miles / 21km: Day Section 11, starting in Aberporth and then following the coast path through lovely Mwnt and along the eastern shore of the Teifi estuary to finish at Cardigan.

On the coast path approaching Llangrannog

A brief history of the Snowdonia & Ceredigion Coast

From prehistory to modern times, signs of human impact change with every turn of the path

Man probably first made an appearance in the Cardigan Bay area towards the end of the last glacial period, about 10,000 years ago. Evidence of Mesolithic people, in the form of flint tools and weapons, has been found on the coast near Aberystwyth. These people would have been hunter-gatherers and, as such, would have had little noticeable impact on the landscape.

Although there is evidence of later peoples — Neolithic and Bronze Age — in parts of Gwynedd and Ceredigion, those walking the coast path will pass very few of these sites. As well as the Mesolithic remains mentioned above, a Bronze Age burial mound has been discovered to the south of Aberystwyth; and, just off route in Dyffryn Ardudwy near Barmouth, is a portal dolmen (double burial chamber) that is thought to be 5,500 years old. This would make it one of the oldest stone structures in the British Isles. But it is really only with the arrival of Celtic tribes that we begin to see a more profound and lasting impact on the landscape. .

These early Celts, who probably came from Brittany between about 500BC and 300BC, brought with them sophisticated farming methods, their own language — a form of which survives in modern Welsh — as well as more warlike behaviour. With fighting within and between clans

Two Neolithic burial chambers above the coast at Dyffryn Ardudwy, Gwynedd

a common occurrence, these Iron Age people built promontory forts all along the coast. The ditches and ramparts of many of them can still be clearly seen on many Ceredigion headlands such as Castell Bach near Cwm Tydu.

Uniting the tribes

The Romans had minimal influence over the Welsh coast, but the Scottish chieftain who first united the tribes of Gwynedd under a single crown was probably the grandson of a high-ranking Roman official. According to the ninth-century Historia Brittonum, Cunedda came to Wales with his eight sons in the early part of the fifth century to crush the Irish tribes that had begun arriving in the fourth century. He originally ruled north and west Wales as a single kingdom, but then granted the southern lands to his son, Ceredig. These became Ceredigion. Today, the administrative regions of Ceredigion and Gwynedd correspond almost exactly with these two early Welsh kingdoms.

In the centuries that followed, the struggle for control over these kingdoms and much of the rest of Wales was often bloody. The Normans arrived in the twelfth century, but, by about 1200, Gwynedd was ruled by Llywelyn the Great, who eventually had control over most of Wales. His son, Dafydd ap Llywelyn, was the first ruler to take on the title Prince of Wales; and his grandson, Llywelyn ap Gruffudd, was effectively the last — although Owain Glyndŵr later assumed the title during his uprising against the English. Llywelyn ap Gruffudd was killed in 1282 during an ambush by Edward I's men at the Battle of Irfon Bridge near Builth Wells in mid-Wales. His death effectively marked the end of Welsh independence.

English rule and Welsh rebellion

Edward I consolidated his rule by bringing in English settlers and building a series of massive castles, including those at Harlech, Conwy, Caernarfon and Beaumaris. See page 72-73 for more on Edward's Gwynedd castles.

There were many attempts to wrest back control from the English over the ensuing decades, but they were all short-lived. The most serious rebellion was that led by Owain Glyndŵr in the early years of the fifteenth century. Having formally assumed his ancestral title of Prince of Powys in 1400, he held court at Harlech in 1404 and set up his parliament in Machynlleth. With his vision of a separate Welsh state, a separate Welsh church and two universities, as well as French backing, he had much support. He gained control over large

Harlech Castle formed part of Edward I's 'Iron Ring'

Saintly gaze: *Saint Carannog's statue overlooks Llangrannog*

areas of Wales, and even briefly bore the title Prince of Wales. But, by 1412, Henry IV had suppressed the uprising.

The power of the church

Christianity came to Wales via missionaries in the fifth and sixth centuries. Religious communities, led by scholarly monks, sprung up. These were known as *llanau*, a word that originally meant simply a plot of land, but later became associated with land with a church on it and, eventually, the church itself. The Welsh place name element, *llan*, is based on this. Villages that grew up around these communities or early churches often used *llan* followed by the name of the priest or saint who established them. Llangrannog, for example, is named after St Carannog and Llanon after St David's mother, St Non.

During the twelfth century, the Cistercians, or White Monks, came to Wales. With the Welsh princes as their patrons, they set up several monasteries, including Strata Florida in Ceredigion. The monks here played an important part, not only in the religious and cultural life of the region, but the political and economic too. They controlled many farms, known as granges, which provided them with food and income; and they became closely tied in with the changing fortunes of their allies. In the early fifteenth century, Henry IV executed some of the monks at Strata Florida for supporting Owain Glyndŵr.

Georgian colour: *The pretty harbour town of Aberaeron*

The power of the sea

The sea has always had a strong influence on the history and economic development of west Wales. It brought raiders, settlers and missionaries. It also brought fish and trade.

Many of the settlements visited by walkers on the Ceredigion coast, including Borth, Aberporth and New Quay, grew up around fishing communities. The herring industry, in particular, was important in the economic development of such places. The fish would either be eaten fresh or prepared for export. The latter would be achieved by smoking the herrings or salting them and then packing them into barrels. Historical records mention the fisheries of Aberystwyth as long ago as the early thirteenth century; and trading figures show Cardigan exporting 1,072 barrels of cured herrings, mostly to London and Dublin, in 1701. Significant numbers of fish were also landed in Gwynedd — at Aberdyfi and Barmouth — but the waters further north were too shallow.

Other exports during the heyday of the ports and harbours of Cardigan Bay included grain, timber, wool and, later, slate from the quarries further inland.

Shipbuilding was another major source of income, with small yards all along the coast of Cardigan Bay and larger bases in harbours such as Barmouth, New Quay and Cardigan. More than 200 boats were built in the five shipyards at Cardigan and St Dogmaels on the Pembrokeshire side of the Teifi estuary. Cardigan was, in fact, one of the most important ports in Wales: in the early nineteenth century, there were three times as many boats registered there as in Swansea.

Combined with the coming of the railways in the nineteenth century, the silting up of many estuarine ports, including Cardigan, marked the end of the golden era of commerce and industry for this coast. But that's not to say the sea's influence over the economic life of the region suddenly ended. Ironically assisted by the arrival of the railways — one of the final nails in the coffin of the ports — tourism began contributing to local coffers during Victorian times. Several resorts sprang up on the Welsh coast, including Fairbourne in Gwynedd, built in the 1890s by Arthur McDougall, owner of the Liverpool flour milling business that later became Rank Hovis McDougall.

Tourism remains an important part of the local economy today with various towns and villages seeing a significant influx of visitors during the spring and summer.

Wildlife along the Snowdonia & Ceredigion Coast

From immense dune systems and salt marshes to cliff-top heathland and wooded cwms, the variety of habitats along the **Snowdonia & Ceredigion Coast** gives rise to an equally wide range of wildlife. You'll never be alone walking this section of the **Wales Coast Path**: whether it's seabirds chattering away on briny, windswept ledges or rare bees that burrow into the sand, your companions will be many and varied. Several of the habitats are recognised and protected as nationally or even internationally important.

Red kite

Western gorse and heather

Sea pinks or 'thrift'

Guillemots

Sea bindweed

Pearl-bordered fritillary

Bottlenose dolphins

Foxglove

Ox-eye daisies

Common lizard

Sand dunes, expansive estuaries & rugged sea cliffs

*The **Snowdonia & Ceredigion** coast's diverse habitats are home to a rich variety of wildlife*

As you walk the coast path, keep your eyes peeled, your mind alert and your binoculars handy: Cardigan Bay has lots to offer both the keen, well-informed naturalist and the casual wildlife observer. From sheer, inaccessible cliffs where vast, noisy seabird colonies can nest without fear of predators to salt marshes, sand dunes, peat bog, woods, heathland and the open sea itself, all home to countless species of birds, fish, mammals, invertebrates, trees and plants, the area is heaving with life — some of it rare. Although it would

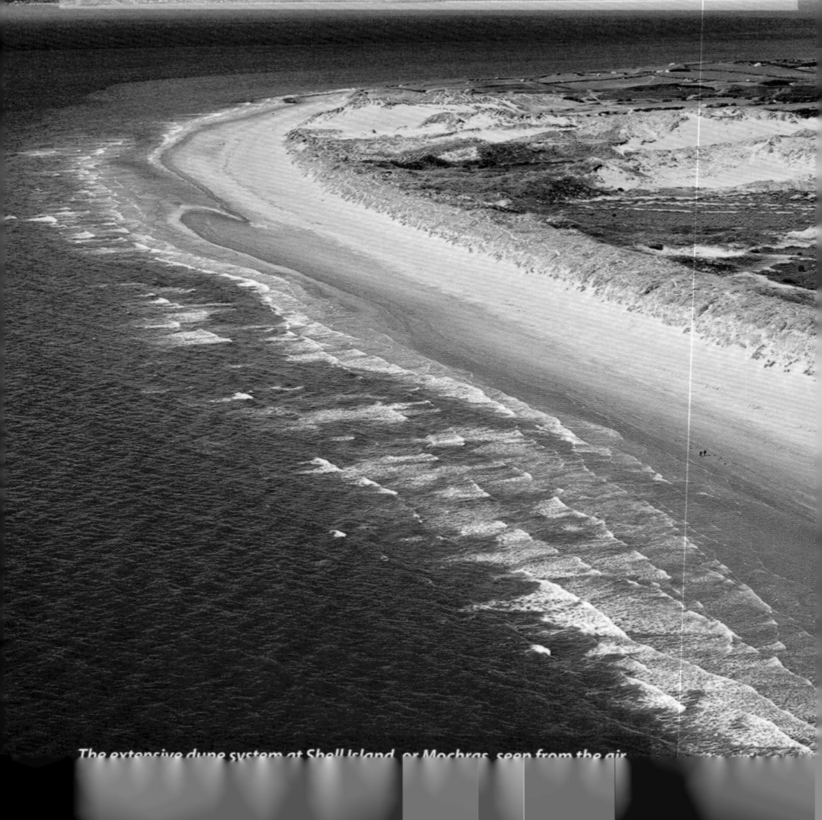

The extensive dune system at Shell Island, or Mochras, seen from the air

be impossible to list all the species you might catch sight of, this chapter provides a guide to some of the most common ones as well as a few of the more elusive characters you may be lucky enough to spot.

A walk of two halves

In so many ways, walking the Cardigan Bay coast from Porthmadog to Cardigan is very much a journey of two contrasting halves. As far as Aberdyfi, as the route skirts the western edge of the Snowdonia National Park through Gwynedd, the scenery is dominated by seemingly never-ending beaches and sand dunes, divided by tidal estuaries where salt marsh and mudflats dominate. Beyond Aberdyfi, the woods, farmland and open hillside on either side of the Afon Dyfi provide an entertaining interlude before walkers reach the cliffs of Ceredigion for a totally different perspective on Cardigan Bay. And, of course, the wildlife reflects these changes.

Birds will undoubtedly be some of your most common companions as you walk from Porthmadog to Cardigan, but the species will differ widely from north to south. The salt marshes and mudflats of the north are important for winter migrants such as pintail, wigeon and whooper swans. Look out too for waders such as redshank, curlew, turnstone, ringed plover and sanderling as they poke about on beaches and mudflats searching for a tasty morsel or two.

Seabirds and raptors

You'll see some of these species in Ceredigion too, but, having reached the cliffs, all your attention is now likely to be diverted to the seabird colonies that nest here during spring and summer. Fulmars, kittiwakes, razorbills, cormorants, shags, common terns, guillemots and a variety of gulls are all reasonably common sights. Offshore stacks such as Birds Rock, near New Quay, are among the favoured nesting sites for many of these birds.

Less common species include choughs, a red-billed, aerobatic member of the crow family. Your best chances of spotting one come during the late summer when the young birds are learning flying skills from their parents. Equally difficult to spot, but often seen in similar cliff-top localities to the chough, is the peregrine falcon. One of the fastest creatures on the planet, watch for a flash of its yellow beak and talons as it goes in for the kill at speeds in excess of 100mph.

Other birds of prey along the Cardigan Bay coast include the endangered hen harrier and the majestic red kite, easily identified by its unmistakeable forked tail. There is even an outside chance of spotting osprey. Still extremely rare in Wales, they have established nesting sites near Porthmadog and

Breeding ospreys nest near Porthmadog each year

Playful acrobats: *Several large pods of bottlenose dolphins live in Cardigan Bay*

Machynlleth in recent years. They tend to return from over-wintering in Africa in early April, and then stay in Wales until September. The Montgomeryshire Wildlife Trust's Dyfi Osprey Project has set up a hide and visitor centre just south of Machynlleth to enable members of the public to view these magnificent, fish-eating birds of prey.

Otters, dolphins and seals

As far as mammals go, you may occasionally spot foxes, stoats, badgers, weasels and roe deer, particularly early or late in the day. Otters are making a comeback in many parts of Britain and are most likely seen on riverbanks and beside lakes at dawn and dusk.

For a better chance of spotting mammals, turn your binoculars towards the sea. The nutrient-rich waters brought by the Gulf Stream allow a range of creatures to thrive in Cardigan Bay, including Atlantic grey seals, harbour porpoises and bottlenose dolphins. They can be seen just about anywhere and at any time along the coast, although the best places for spotting dolphins and porpoises are probably New Quay, Aberporth and Mwnt. Numbers increase during the summer and early autumn, reaching a peak in September and October. Several companies offer boat-based wildlife watching tours from New Quay, Cardigan and Barmouth during the summer. (See page 135 for more on bottlenose dolphins.)

Born to the sea: *Atlantic grey seal pups are born with distinctive white coats*

At low tide, grey seals often haul out on the rocks and beaches in the Cwmtydu area and around Cardigan Island. From August through to the late autumn, females begin arriving on sheltered beaches and in some of the larger sea caves along the Welsh coast to give birth to their pups, which are covered in soft white fur for the first few weeks of their lives. December to February is a good time to spot seals. This is when large numbers of adults congregate on beaches to moult.

The dunes of Gwynedd and the cliffs of Ceredigion support a wide range of wildflowers. The late spring and early summer are probably the best times to enjoy this colourful spectacle. The most common, and easily identifiable species are bluebells, ox-eye daisies, thrift and sea campion, but watch too for the yellow burst associated with tormentil and birdsfoot trefoil. More unusual wildflowers, including several species of orchid, dwell among the shifting dunes of Morfa Harlech and Morfa Dyffryn.

The dunes — as well as the heathland vegetation — hide a number of reptiles. Some, such as the sand lizard, are very localised, while others, including common lizards, slow worms, grass snakes and adders, are spread widely. Don't be alarmed if you stumble across any of them: the only one that can hurt you is the adder. Britain's only venomous snake, the adder will usually make itself scarce as soon as it senses your approach. They bite only as a last resort: if you tread on one or try to pick one up. Even then, for most people, the worst symptoms of an adder bite are likely to be nausea and severe bruising. It's a different story for our canine friends though: if you're bringing your dog on the trail, be aware that an adder bite can kill.

With the wide variety of habitats all along the Cardigan Bay coast, there's plenty to keep lepidopterists entertained too — from dune-based butterflies to woodland varieties. The valley of the Afon Soden, southwest of New Quay, is particularly well-known for its butterflies and moths. The National Trust carries out work here to ensure the survival of several species, including the pearl-bordered fritillary.

Protected sites

Complementing the efforts of organisations such as the National Trust and the Wildlife Trusts, many of the habitats and landscapes along the Cardigan Bay coast receive statutory protection. Almost all of the northern section of the route — from the moment the route crosses the Afon Dwyryd near Porthmadog to the Afon Dyfi near Machynlleth — is within the Snowdonia National Park and, as such, receives some of the highest levels of protection afforded to landscapes and heritage in the UK.

Then, just a few miles beyond the National Park boundary, walkers enter one of only 11 areas in the UK designated by UNESCO as an international Biosphere Reserve: the Dyfi Biosphere. Made up of the mudflats of the Dyfi estuary, the Ynyslas dunes and the huge raised peat bog of Cors Fochno at Borth, the area is recognised for maintaining a balanced, sustainable relationship between nature and people.

Special Areas of Conservation (SAC), protected under European law, have also been set up, including the Cardigan Bay SAC. This stretches from Aberarth in Ceredigion to Ceibwr Bay in Pembrokeshire, extending almost 20 kilometres out to sea and providing specific protection for bottlenose dolphins, lampreys, grey seals, reefs, sandbanks and sea caves. In addition, there are several National Nature Reserves and many Sites of Special Scientific Interest, each of which has been recognised for particular habitats or species.

Of course, this can only be a brief summary of the range of wildlife that may be encountered along this section of the Wales Coast Path. For further details about the region's natural heritage, check out the Natural Resources Wales website at **www.naturalresourceswales.gov.uk**.

Day Sections

1.	Porthmadog to Harlech	*11 miles/ 19 kilometres*
2.	Harlech to Barmouth	*17 miles/ 27 kilometres*
3.	Barmouth to Llwyngwril	*8 miles/ 14 kilometres*
4.	Llwyngwril to Aberdyfi	*12 miles/ 19 kilometres*
5.	Aberdyfi to Machynlleth	*12 miles/ 19 kilometres*
6.	Machynlleth to Borth	*18 miles/ 29 kilometres*
7.	Borth (or Ynyslas) to Aberystwyth	*6 miles/ 10 kilometres*
8.	Aberystwyth to Llanon	*13 miles/ 21 kilometres*
9.	Llanon to New Quay	*11 miles/ 18 kilometres*
10.	New Quay to Aberporth	*13 miles/ 21 kilometres*
11.	Aberporth to Cardigan	*13 miles/ 21 kilometres*

Snowdonia & Ceredigion Coast

section of the Wales Coast Path

Includes the complete

Ceredigion Coast Path

www.ceredigioncoastpath.org.uk

On the coast path near Llangrannog *(Day Section 10)*

Porthmadog to Harlech

Distance: *19 kilometres / 11 miles* | **Start:** *Western end of road bridge (A497) over Afon Glaslyn, Porthmadog Harbour SH 570 384* | **Finish:** *Harlech Railway Station SH 580 313* | **Maps:** *OS Explorer OL18 Harlech, Porthmadog and Bala, Landranger 124 Porthmadog and Dolgellau*

Outline: A day of meandering through woodland and beside wildlife-rich estuaries along the western edge of the Snowdonia National Park.

After leaving Porthmadog, the route sets off across farmland and through woodland north of Portmeirion before embarking on a 3.7-kilometre stretch of road walking. Having crossed the new Pont Briwet, salt marshes and tidal creeks become the order of the day — heaven for bird enthusiasts, particularly in the winter when a wide variety of wildfowl fly in from the north. The section ends with easy, level walking along tracks and field paths to reach the historic town of Harlech, famous for its imposing castle.

Services: *Porthmadog has a good range of facilities, including accommodation, places to eat, cash machines, shops and public toilets. There are also places to stay and to eat, shops, cash machine and public toilets in Penrhyndeudraeth and in Harlech. Like many stretches of the path through Gwynedd, this section passes several stations on the Cambrian Coast railway line, providing points at which the day could be cut short. Ralio Rownd, Penrhyndeudraeth | 07950 176551*

Don't miss: **Ffestiniog and Welsh Highland Railways** – heritage railway lines | **Portmeirion** – Italianate village | **Afon Dwyryd estuary** – winter feeding ground for waders and wildfowl

▲ *Portmeirion from the air*

Porthmadog

Before 1811, the land that Porthmadog now stands upon was under water. It was only after William Madocks, an MP and entrepreneur, bought up land nearby that the idea of the town was born. He slowly began extending his property by building embankments to reclaim land from the estuary. After building a settlement at Tremadog, he then set his sights on building a causeway across the mouth of the Afon Glaslyn. Now known as The Cob, this was completed in 1811, although it had to be repaired after it was breached by a massive storm the following year.

The construction of The Cob and the diversion of the Afon Glaslyn resulted in the creation of a new harbour. By the middle of the 1820s, this was being used by ocean-going vessels of up to 60 tons, and the town of Porthmadog was growing up around it. During the 1830s, the Ffestiniog Railway and other tramways started bringing slate down to the harbour from the mines and quarries in the mountains, and it was this trade that really prompted the growth of the town — from a population of just a few hundred in 1821 to more than 3,000 according to the 1861 census.

Yachts in the harbour at Porthmadog

Looking inland: *The mountains of Snowdonia seen from the Cob, Porthmadog*

The route: **Porthmadog to Harlech**

1 Standing at the western end of the **road bridge** over the **Afon Glaslyn** and with your back to **Porthmadog's harbour**, turn right along the A497, immediately crossing the river. You'll see the **Harbour Station of the Ffestiniog and Welsh Highland Railways** on your right.

The Ffestiniog Railway was built to serve the slate industry, climbing more than 200m on its 21-kilometre journey from Porthmadog to Blaenau Ffestiniog at the foot of Snowdonia's mountains. When it was first built, in the 1830s, trains ran down from the quarries by gravity, the empty wagons then being pulled back up into the hills by horses. The line was converted to steam in 1863.

Cross over in a short while to pick up the combined cycle path and pedestrian walkway running to the left of the road. Together with the narrow-gauge **Ffestiniog line**, the road and multi-use path cross the estuary on **The Cob**.

2 Having crossed, you'll see a parking layby on your left. Immediately after this, take the lane rising to the right of the main road. Bear left along the railway track for a few strides and then carefully cross it to go through the small gate on the other side. A pleasant path now climbs through the trees. Keep right at an early fork. Soon after the wooded path turns sharp left,

you'll go through a gate to enter a field. Now turn sharp right, heading up the slope — aiming to the right of the farm buildings at the top of the rise. On reaching a large gate, don't go through it; instead, turn left to walk with the fence on your right. Go through a gate to the left of some buildings and then keep straight on — along a rough track. Turn right just before a cattle grid. Having gone through a couple of gates, the path reaches the edge of **Portmeirion**.

'The Powder Works'

Gwaith Powdwr was once Europe's largest explosives factory. The production of guncotton started in 1872 and, during World War One, ICI set up a munitions operation here. After the world wars, the plant continued producing explosives for the mining industry, but it lost most of its UK markets after the pit closures of the 1980s. The factory closed in 1995. The site is now a nature reserve that is home to nightjars, pied flycatchers, adders and lesser horseshoe bats.

There's no access to walkers from here, so the path now swings left. After a gate, the way ahead is less clear; keep reasonably close to the fence on the left. Beyond the next gate, you'll join a rough lane close to the house at **Plas Canol**. Follow this for about 180 metres and then turn right in front of some derelict farm buildings. Entering a field, walk with the fence on your left.

The next gate provides access to another woodland path. Ignore the trail to the right early on; simply follow the main path until you reach a surfaced lane.

3 This is **Portmeirion**'s driveway, so if you wish to visit the fascinating village, you should turn right here to walk the 850 metres to the ticket office.

The whimsical Italianate retreat of Portmeirion was built over a 50-year period, starting in 1925, by architect Clough Williams-Ellis. During the 1960s, its colourful buildings, secret archways and rhododendron-filled gardens became the surreal setting for the cult TV series The Prisoner, starring Patrick McGoohan.

Those wishing to push on along the Coast Path will cross over and follow the lane downhill on the other side, soon to be greeted by a magnificent view across the estuary of the Afon Dwyryd. Turn left at the next junction and then, having walked the track for about 200 metres, go through the small gate on the right. Walk down the field with a fence on your right and

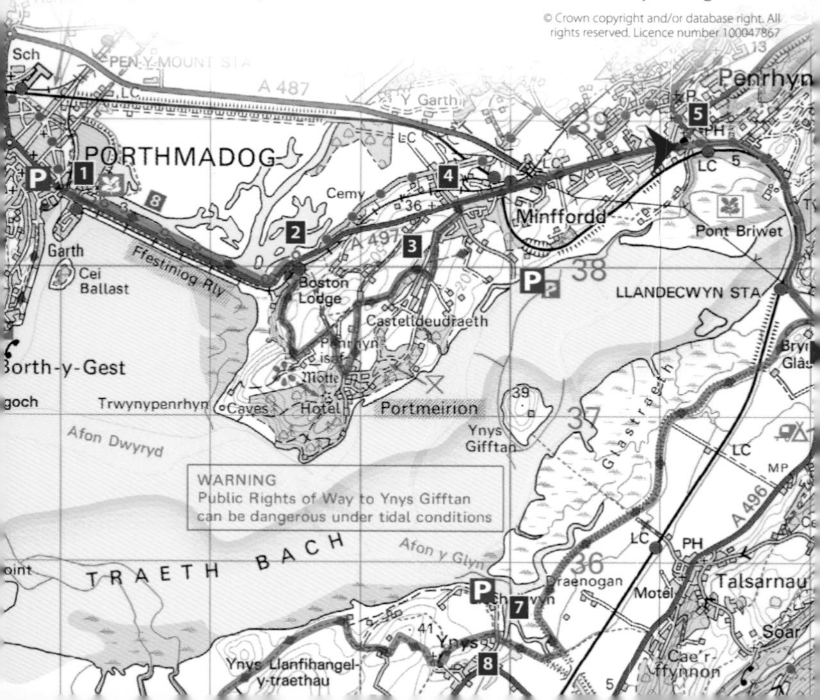

Summer scene: *Portmeirion is a popular tourist attraction*

then follow the boundary round to the left. Beyond the farm gate, turn left along the minor road through **Minffordd**.

4 Turn right when you reach the **A497**. You now follow the main road all the way to **Penrhyndeudraeth**, keeping straight on at a roundabout close to a business park (where it becomes the **A487**). It's about 1.7 kilometres, but there is pavement almost all the way.

5 Entering **Penrhyndeudraeth**, turn right at the main crossroads in the village, signposted to 'Harlech'. At the T-junction — opposite **Penrhyndeudraeth Station** — turn left. The ground to the left of the road here was the site of the Gwaith Powdwr explosives factory. The road crosses the **Afon Dwyryd** via the new **Pont Briwet**.

The original timber road and rail bridge across the Afon Dwyryd, built in the 1860s, was too narrow for pedestrians. Up until July 2015, when the new £20 million bridge was opened, people walking the Wales Coast Path from Porthmadog to Harlech had to head inland to cross the river at Maentwrog — a detour of about 16 kilometres.

6 About 300 metres after passing to the left of **Llandecwyn Station**, take the surfaced track on the right. Just before the last house, go through a small gate and then continue through the field with the boundary on your left. Having climbed a stile in the fence next to the railway, carefully cross the

A steam train crossing the Cob at Porthmadog

Heritage railways

Journey back to the age of steam

There are about a dozen heritage railways in Wales, six of which start from settlements along this section of the Wales Coast Path. Although they are now popular tourist attractions, most trace their roots back to the mineral industries of the nineteenth and early twentieth centuries. The Talyllyn Railway, for example, which terminates at Tywyn, was built in the mid-1860s to serve the Bryn Eglwys slate quarry, while the Vale of Rheidol Railway, between Aberystwyth and Devil's Bridge, was opened in 1902, largely to breathe fresh life into the area's lead mines and to carry timber for pit props in the coal mines of South Wales.

Some of these lines have to overcome all sorts of natural obstacles. The engines of the Ffestiniog Railway have to climb more than 200 metres on their 22-kilometre journey from Porthmadog to Blaenau Ffestiniog. Right from the outset, where the railway passes over a 1,500 metre-long stone causeway that has been holding back the sea since 1811, the engineering feats are apparent. They include impressive cuttings, steep embankments and a 670 metre-long tunnel blasted through the mountains.

More information: For a list of all the scenic railways and web links to each, go to: www.visitwales.com

tracks and the stile on the other side. Now walk along the top of the embankment with the **Afon Dwyryd** on your right. As you make your way along the embankment, crossing countless stiles, you'll eventually see Portmeirion on the other side of the water and Harlech Castle in the distance.

The estuary here, with its dreamy, far-reaching views, consists largely of sand flats and salt marsh. In winter, it becomes an important feeding ground for a wide variety of wildfowl, including large numbers of pintail ducks. The island on the eastern side of the channel is Ynys Gifftan, or 'Anne's gift island'.

7 Having followed the estuary path for 2.4 kilometres, it makes a decisive bend to the left and goes through a gate. You have now lost the fence on your right. In a few more metres — just before the next stile — turn right, crossing damp ground to reach the **footbridge over the Afon Glyn**. Having crossed, bear right along the path beside the **salt marsh**. After going through a gate to the left of a former warehouse at **Ynys**, turn right along the lane.

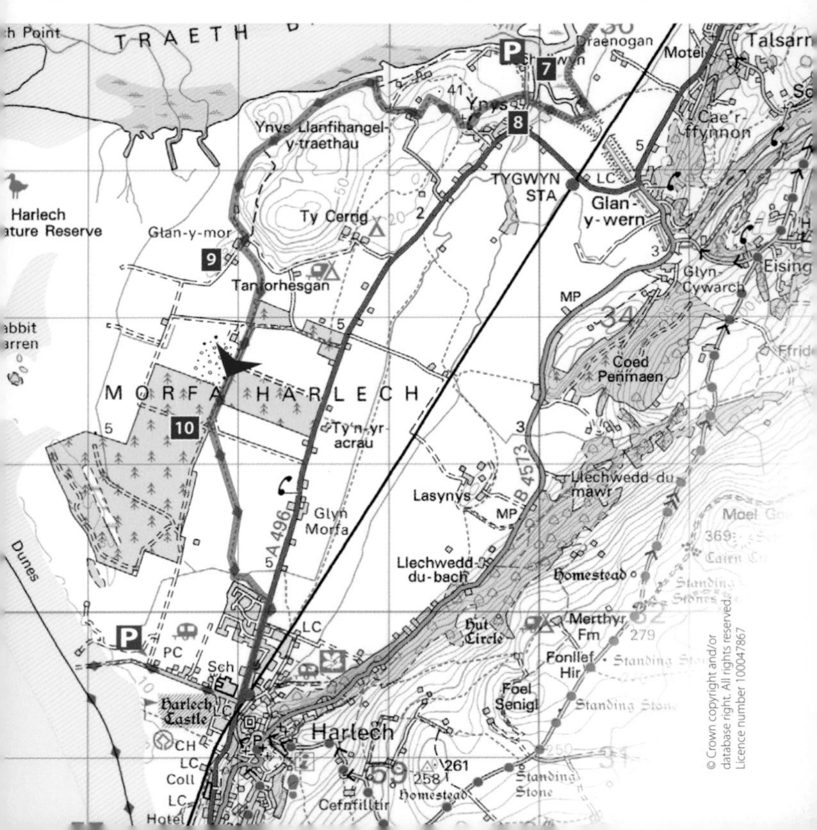

Tidal sands: *Looking across the Dwyryd estuary towards Portmeirion at low tide*

This area served as Harlech's port and a shipbuilding centre until 1806 when the Enclosure Act resulted in the reclamation of more salt marsh and the closure of this part of the estuary. Before this time, it is thought there might have been a canal running from the castle to Ynys.

8 Almost immediately, go through the gate on the left — on to a grassy track between low walls. Entering a field, keep the wall on your left and then, after a wooden gate in the field corner, continue in the same direction but now with a hedgerow on your right. After a small gate, walk gently uphill towards the wall of **St Michael's churchyard**. Swing left, keeping this high wall on your right. Cross the church's access lane and then continue beside the wall until you see some steps on your left. Descend these and then, beyond a flat, grassy interlude, climb the steps on the other side.

Ynys means 'island' and, when it was first established, St Michael's Church would have occupied a tidal islet, accessible only by boat at high tide. The building that stands today dates mainly from the second half of the nineteenth century, although a carved stone outside the church's west door suggests an earlier chapel was built here in the twelfth century.

After a gate, head uphill through the bracken towards a waymarker post.

Continuing uphill, turn right at the next waymarker. Keep the wall on your left, following it round two bends, until you near a building at **Cefn-gwyn**. Now veer right to reach a kissing-gate. Once through this, drop to the track and turn right along it — through the gate. At a fork, bear left. The track leads to an isolated house, called **Clogwyn Melyn**, at the edge of the salt marsh. *Before the original Pont Briwet opened in the 1860s, those wishing to travel across the water to Porthmadog would've caught the ferry from here.* Take the path

Ynys Gifftan

Situated in the Afon Dwyryd estuary, Ynys Gifftan, or 'Anne's gift island', was given to a descendant of the current Lord Harlech by Queen Anne in the early 1700s with the caveat that it could never be sold. Little more than 400 metres wide, it is home to a single uninhabited cottage. It can only be reached at low tide, an 800-metre wet walk from Talsarnau railway station.

left. This keeps close to the edge of the estuary, providing uninterrupted views across to Portmeirion.

After a gap in an old wall, the faint, grassy trail heads up through the bracken. It then goes through a kissing-gate in the fence on your right before continuing in roughly the same direction as before. The route now passes through an area of hillocks to reach yet another small gate. Bearing right and then quickly left, keep to the right of the steep, bracken-covered slope. To the right now is a vast expanse of flat wetland, leading up to the dunes.

After the next kissing-gate, bear half-left to pass in front of a solitary grey house (**Glan-y-morfa**). Another kissing-gate leads on to a rough track along which you turn left. At the next track junction, bear right — heading into the farmyard at **Glan-y-mor** and passing to the left of the house. On exiting the farmyard, turn left immediately — through another kissing-gate.

9 Cross the field diagonally. After the next gate, continue diagonally across this larger field and you'll find a kissing-gate in the far corner. Go through this and walk with the fence on your immediate left. Cross the **recycling centre**'s driveway, go through the gap in the gorse opposite and then through the fence to pick up a concrete track. This follows a straight line between stands of small trees.

10 Just after passing and ignoring another surfaced track to the right, go through the kissing-gate on the left. A faint trail through the grass indicates the line you take across this field. Maintain exactly the same line across the next two fields too.

Walkers on the vast expanse of Harlech beach

Vantage point: *Harlech Castle sits high above the coastal plain*

Harlech Castle, sitting atop its rocky perch, dominates the scene ahead. In the time of Edward I, when it was built, it would've been even more prominent — as it was rendered and painted white.

On reaching the far side of the third and largest field, don't be tempted to go through the farm gate; instead bear half-right to walk with the fence on your left.

Leave the field via a **footbridge** and then go through a kissing-gate to enter a copse. The faint trail winds its way through the trees, over a gated footbridge and beside a drainage ditch. It makes its way over to some houses on the **edge of Harlech**. As it does so, watch for a small metal gate on the right. Once through this, follow the path between the homes to reach a quiet, residential road. Turn left along this and, when it bends sharp right, follow the trail through the gorse to the left of the asphalt to reach the **A496**. Turn right along the main road to reach the entrance to Harlech Station. Today's section of the Wales Coast Path ends here, but to reach the **main part of Harlech**, continue over the level crossing and take the road climbing to the left — a cruelly steep way to end what is almost a 19-kilometre walk.

Round towers and concentric walls at Harlech Castle

An 'Iron Ring' of castles

Edward I's 'finest examples' of military architecture

When Edward I gained control over Wales in the late thirteenth century, he embarked on one of medieval Europe's most ambitious building projects. He strengthened castles built or captured by his late father, Henry III. On Cardigan Bay, these included Aberystwyth and Cardigan. But he also had plans of his own: realising that the biggest threat to his rule came from north Wales, he created an 'iron ring' of mighty fortresses. These were strategically located and used the most advanced military architecture of the age.

The four most significant were in Gwynedd — at Conwy, Harlech, Caernarfon and Beaumaris. Designed by the Savoy architect, James of St George, they used a combination of concentric defences, barbicans and large gatehouses. Each of the castles was planned with

Caernarfon Castle's octagonal towers

its own walled *bastide* town, based on settlements in Edward's French duchy of Gascony. The towns were populated solely by English settlers; the Welsh were banned from living inside the walls, and were only allowed to enter, unarmed, during daylight hours. To build Beaumaris on Anglesey, the Welsh population of a nearby town was evicted and moved 19 kilometres from the new English settlement

Conwy, Caernarfon, Beaumaris and even Harlech at the time were all ports, which meant they could be supplied from the sea. This was put to the test for the first time in 1295 when Madog ap Llywelyn led a rebellion against English rule. Both Harlech and Conwy were besieged, but never fell to the Welsh — thanks in part to coastal supply routes.

"Exploring castles in Wales ranks as the number one must-do activity for overseas visitors to Britain."

Visit Britain

Only the castles at Conwy and Harlech were completed: the costs had proved too much for Edward. He'd employed only the best architects and masons, and armies of labourers had to be brought in from England to do the work. By 1304, he'd spent at least £80,000 on his building programme throughout Wales. With his attention and money increasingly focussed on his wars with the Scots,

Beaumaris is the most advanced of Edward I's 'Iron Ring' castles

funds were short. Caernarfon Castle remained incomplete and the walls at Beaumaris Castle never reached their intended height.

Despite the vision never quite coming to full fruition, these four castles are today recognised by UNESCO as being the "finest examples of late thirteenth century and early fourteenth century military architecture in Europe". Known collectively as 'the castles and town walls of King Edward in Gwynedd', they became a World Heritage site in 1986, joining a list of elite landmarks that includes India's Taj Mahal and the Great Wall of China.

More information: For more details, see: www.unesco.org

Harlech to Barmouth

Distance: *27 kilometres / 17 miles* | **Start:** *Harlech Railway Station SH 580 313* | *Finish: Barmouth Harbour SH 615 154* | **Maps:** *Ordnance Survey Explorer OL18 Harlech, Porthmadog and Bala, Landranger 124 Porthmadog and Dolgellau*

Outline: Wildlife-rich wetlands and two long beaches backed by immense dune systems are crossed on a day linking Harlech and Barmouth.

After leaving Harlech, the vast beaches and shifting dunes of Morfa Harlech and Morfa Dyffryn are undoubtedly the highlights of section two, home to an often unusual variety of wildlife as well as some magnificent views. Keep your binoculars handy as you cross estuarine wetlands and reed marshes where rare birds might be encountered. Between the nature reserves, the route uses a combination of mostly quiet lanes, field paths and riverside trails. The final few kilometres include a long section beside a main road.

Services: *Harlech and Barmouth have a good range of facilities, including accommodation, places to eat, cash machines, shops and public toilets. There are other places to stay and to eat along this section, including campsites at Shell Island and Tal-y-bont. Public toilets and seasonal café at Llandanwg. As on the previous day, this section passes several stations on the Cambrian Coast line, providing points at which the route could be cut short. Blue Line Cabs, Barmouth | 07585 855243*

Don't miss: **Harlech Castle** – substantial thirteenth-century ruins | **St Tanwg's** – simple church almost swallowed by dunes | **Morfa Harlech and Morfa Dyffryn** – beaches, dunes and wildlife

▲ *Aerial view of Shell Island*

Harlech

Harlech is dominated by the medieval castle that sits on top of an almost vertical cliff-face. It was built by Edward I in the late thirteenth century as part of his 'iron ring' of fortresses, a very visible reminder to the Welsh of England's might. It was probably whitewashed in Edward's day, a formidable-looking apparition looming over the coast. One of the castle's most unusual features is the secret, 61 metre-long stairway that still leads from the castle walls to the base of the cliff on which it stands. This gave castle dwellers access to the sea — via a channel — and crucial supplies during times of siege.

The castle has seen much action in its long lifetime. It was taken by the Welsh leader Owain Glyndŵr in 1404 and served as his headquarters until 1409 when it was recaptured by English troops led by the future King Henry V. It became one of the last Lancastrian strongholds during the Wars of the Roses, finally falling to a Yorkist siege in 1468. Then, in 1647, it was the last Royalist castle to fall to Oliver Cromwell, bringing an end to the first part of the English Civil War.

Visitors can still explore the castle's massive east gatehouse and become totally disorientated in the maze of dark stairways leading up to the battlements.

The sea once reached the foot of Harlech Castle's crag

The Route: **Harlech to Barmouth**

1 Starting the day in the shadow of **Harlech Castle**, and with your back to the lane leading up to **Harlech Station**, turn left along the **A496** and immediately right along a minor road signposted to the beach and recycling centre. You'll quickly pass a small grocery store on the left and, later, a couple of caravan sites. The road ends at a car park with public toilets in it. Keep straight ahead, through the gate, to access a broad, surfaced track which leads through the dunes and down to **Harlech Beach**.

Finally, after a day of walking through woods and beside estuaries, we've reached the coast proper. And what a marvellous section of coast it is! The vast, empty beach stretches on for miles, and the views, both across the water to the Llŷn peninsula and inland towards the mountains of Snowdonia, are truly spellbinding.

The dunes here are protected as part of the Morfa Harlech National Nature Reserve. They are 'shifting' dunes, constantly being reshaped and not stable enough to allow plants such as marram grass to take a hold. This creates an unusual habitat that is home to a number of rare species, including the mining

Church in the dunes: *Wind-blown sand threatens to bury tiny St Tanwg's Church at Llandanwg*

bee which burrows into the sand to build its nest. Sand lizards have recently been reintroduced, and the reserve is also known for its impressive wildflower displays in the spring and summer, including a large variety of orchids.

2 Turn left and walk along the beach for about 1.6 kilometres. When the dunes end, continue below the wall of the railway for a further 120 metres — to reach a **set of steps**. Some of the boulders between the dunes and the steps will be covered for about 45 minutes either side of high tide, so you may have to wait a while. Once up the steps, carefully cross the **railway line** and the stile opposite to begin climbing the zig-zags. The ascent is steep, but the reward comes in the form of some excellent views.

At the top of the main climb, the path goes through a gate and then continues more gently uphill to reach the **A496**. Turn right and walk along the grass verge and then the pavement for about 200 metres. Take the first road on the right — signposted to 'Llandanwg'. The road crosses the railway close to **Llandanwg Station** and ends at a **car park** with **public toilets** and **seasonal café**.

The tiny church at Llandanwg is dedicated to St Tanwg, who is thought to have established a chapel here in the fifth century. The building that exists today is medieval, with a thirteenth-century nave, but the site contains inscribed stones dating back to St Tanwg's time. Most of the churchyard is buried beneath the dunes.

Mountain backdrop: *The hills of Snowdonia stop just short of the coast*

3 Leave the road just before it enters the car park. As it swings right, take the track to the left and then, almost immediately, go through the gate on the right, a National Trust sign welcoming you to **Y Maes**. Keep straight ahead, walking with a reed-filled ditch on your left. Follow this round to the left and then cross it via a bridge. On the other side, go through the gate and bear right along the top of a raised embankment along the edge of **Pensarn Harbour**.

A few leisure boats bop up and down on the waters of Pensarn Harbour while waders poke about in the mud flats for a bite to eat. Little egrets are an increasingly common sight. These white heron-like birds are slowing making their way north through the UK after first breeding on England's south coast in 1996.

Just before the railway, drop right to cross a small **wooden bridge**. Follow a faint path towards the river and then over to a small group of buildings at the water's edge — the **Christian Mountain Centre**'s outdoor pursuits base. Go through a gate to enter the yard of the buildings, pass beneath two arches and then follow the access lane to the left. Cross the railway tracks again, close to **Pensarn Station**, and then turn right along the road.

4 You'll have to walk along the grass verge at first, but the path then drops through a small gate and continues just below the level of the asphalt. After the next gate, turn right — away from the road — and make for the black-and-white railed footbridge over the **Afon Artro**. Once across, turn left along the top of a raised embankment. *Watch for dippers on the rocks as you follow the river upstream.* After a gate, enter a parking area and turn right along a surfaced path that runs parallel with a minor road.

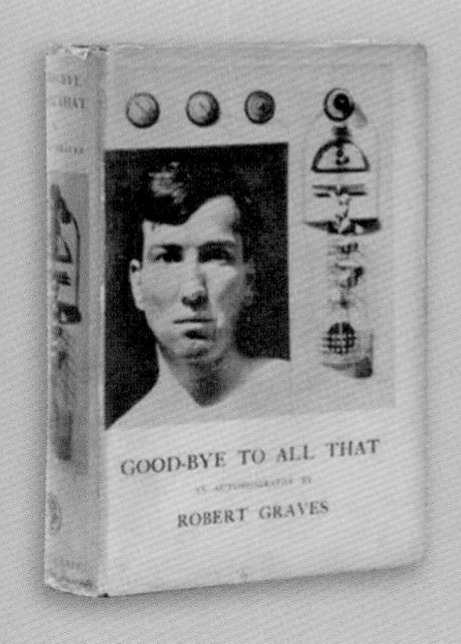

Robert Graves

As a child, the writer Robert Graves spent family holidays near Harlech, and the area left a lasting impression on him. His 1929 autobiography Goodbye to All That *includes descriptions of the town, and many of his poems are inspired by the local landscape. From 1929 until his death in 1985, he lived on Mallorca, but even here he sought out a place "as near as possible to the scenery I was accustomed to in Harlech".*

5 Reaching the road, turn right, soon crossing back over the railway close to **Llanbedr Station**. The road passes **Llanbedr Aviation Centre** and makes its way towards the mudflats. The public road becomes a private road — belonging to **Shell Island** — at a sharp bend to the left. Just before this, go through a small gate on the left to set out along a raised trail across a substantial area of wetland. The grasses slowly give way to reeds and then stunted woodland.

Eventually, as you near the dunes of **Morfa Dyffryn**, you'll hit a T-junction with a wider track. Turn right here. Soon after passing, and ignoring, a turning to the right, follow the track round to the right. It's not always obvious because the sand, blown off the dunes, obscures it in places. Soon after a sharp bend to the right, take a narrower track on the left and then drop on to another stretch of what seems like never-ending beach, part of which is popular with naturists.

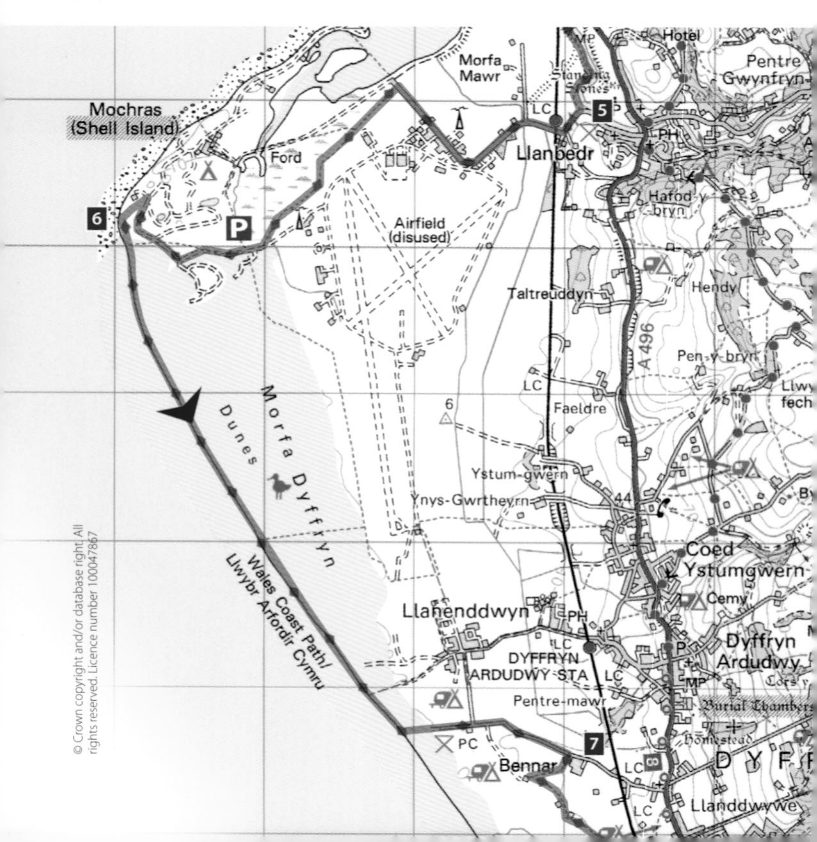

Safe haven: *Yachts and cruisers moored in Pensarn Harbour*

Like Morfa Harlech further north, the dunes of Morfa Dyffryn are constantly shifting, providing a habitat for many species of wildlife, including a vast array of fungi in the autumn and wild orchids that bring a splash of colour in spring and summer. The endangered hen harrier has been known to roost in a small area of reeds here, and migratory waders include ringed plover, turnstone and sanderling. The latter can be seen in large flocks that seem to act as a single unit. They fly low over the beach, suddenly land at the water's edge, rush around madly, plunging their many beaks into the sand in search of a tasty meal and then, just as abruptly, take to the air again to restart the process further down the strand.

6 Turn left and walk along this immense beach for about 4 kilometres, turning round from time to time to enjoy spectacular views across the bay to the hills of the Llŷn peninsula. Sand runs right up to the dunes for most of the way, but when you see pebbles at the back of the beach, you know you're nearing the point at which you leave this wonderful stretch of the walk. Watch for a red-and-white striped pole (SH 569 226) and, from here, you'll find a **boardwalk** that runs back through the dunes.

After passing the **car park** and **public toilets** near **Bennar**, keep following the lane inland — with the prominent, rounded hill of Moelfre ahead and to the left.

Kit off?: *A signed section of Morfa Dyffryn is one of Wales' designated official Naturist Beaches*

7 A few hundred metres after passing the entrance to a caravan site, watch for a few houses to the right of the asphalt. Just before these, go through a small gate on the right. Head up the field, parallel with a wall on the left. After a stile, keep to the right of the wall straight ahead for about 50 metres and then swing right — crossing the field to another stile next to a power pole. Once over this, walk in the general direction of the two-storey house and then cross the stile next to the farm gate on the left.

Bear left, passing just to the left of solitary barn and then continue on to the next group of farm buildings. Turn right to walk with the fence-topped wall on your left. Follow this round to the left and then left again to reach a metal farm gate. Once through the gate, turn right, to walk diagonally across the field. After the next stile, veer slightly right to reach a wall corner with a waymarker on it. Continuing in the same direction, go through a large gate and then bear right, to walk beside the wall on your right. After the stile in the field corner, continue for a few more metres to reach a grassy track close to the **Afon Ysgethin**.

Turn right along the track. Just before the next gate, veer left and follow the trail down to the **river**. Having crossed the **footbridge**, you enter a

small **campsite**. Keep straight ahead, walking parallel with the line of trees on your left. You'll join a stony track to the right of a static caravan. Exit the field on this and then, just after passing **Dalar**'s tiny farmhouse, turn right through one gate. Immediately go right again to pass around the back of the farmhouse and then go left - along a path between a fence and a wall.

Soon after the next small gate, **another campsite** is entered. Keep close to the fence and hedgerow on the left and then continue in the same direction

Orchids at Morfa Dyffryn

Wild orchids bring a splash of colour to the Morfa Dyffryn National Nature Reserve in spring and summer. They tend to grow in the dune slacks, the flat areas between the dunes that are submerged in rainwater in winter and retain some of this moisture in summer. Species include the marsh helleborine, the northern marsh orchid, the early marsh orchid and, less common, the green-flowered helleborine and fen orchid.

Endless sand: *Morfa Dyffryn's vast dune system is a priceless wildlife habitat*

on a stony track. Bear right along the holiday park's surfaced lane. Follow this round to the left and out on to a minor road

8 To reach **Tal-y-bont Station**, turn left along this road. The Wales Coast Path, on the other hand, goes right and immediately left through a small gate. Walk with the wall on your right and then go through a small gate in the wall ahead. You'll now see two gates, about 20 metres apart, on the other side of the field. Go through the one on the right and then walk with the wall on your left. After a stile, follow the gravel track beside a caravan site and round to the left. Turn right and immediately fork left.

Carefully cross the railway line and then go through a large metal gate to your right. Walk beside the fence on your right. Having crossed two small enclosures, a kissing-gate leads into a third, larger enclosure. Continuing in roughly the same direction, make your way to a ladder stile just to the right of a field gate. Having climbed this, make your way towards the house — **Sebonig**. A stile in the garden wall, not obvious from a distance, provides access to the gravel yard. Walk directly in front of the house, cross another stile in a wall and then turn left — through a small gate and up the side of the field to reach the road.

Llanddwywe
Pont-Fadog
Llecheiddior
Cairns
Tal-y-bont
Eithin-fynydd
Cairn
Hendre Fechan
Hengwm
Sebonig
Pen y Dinas
Homestead
Carneddau Hengwm
Cairn Circle
Egryn Abbey
Mynydd Egryn
Trawsdir
Is Mynydd
Llwynwccws Fm
Plas canol
Llwyndu Fm
Hotel
Bodfan
Llanaber
Fort
Bwlch y Llan
Ffridd y Graig
Gellfawr
Plas Mynach
Garn
Gorllwyn
Panorama Walk
BARMOUTH/ ABERMAW
Dinas Oleu
Coes-faen
Mus LB Sta
Mus Harbour
Ferry P (Summer only)
Ynys y Brawd
Barmouth Bridge
North Bank
Y Perch
Foot Br (Toll)
Cerrig y Gorllwyn
Fegla Fawr
Fairbourne Railway
The Bar
MORFA MAWDDACH
Cerrig Arthur
A 496

Sun and sea: *The vast sandy beach and promenade at Barmouth*

9 Turn right along the **A496**. A long section of road walking now follows as you head past the **Norbar** (formerly The Wayside pub) and into **Llanaber** — 4 kilometres in total. There is pavement all the way, and the views of both hills and sea will help to relieve the tedium.

In the eighteenth century, various sites in Llanaber were used by smugglers to store contraband, including illegally imported alcohol. Legend has it that table tombs in the churchyard were among their many hiding places.

10 About 800 metres after passing the turning for **Llanaber Station** — down to the right — watch for a **postbox** in the wall on the right. Immediately after the next house, head steeply down a surfaced path on the right — signposted to the 'beach'. This crosses the **railway** to come out at the end of **Barmouth's promenade**. Turn left and follow this walkway into town. If the tide's out, you'll be able to walk on the beach; if the tide is in and it's a rough day, you may need to walk in the road from time to time as the waves crash over the sea wall.

This isn't the most pleasant way to approach **Barmouth**, but once you've passed all the grey housing and the amusement arcades, you'll reach the considerably more attractive **harbour**. The road bends round to the left here and you're now able to look across the lovely Mawddach estuary, crossed by the impressive **Barmouth Bridge** and backed by dramatic mountain scenery that includes the 893m Cadair Idris. Follow the road along the water's edge — passing Davy Jones' Locker, housed in **Tŷ Gwyn**, one of the town's oldest buildings. Continue until you reach the point at which the railway crosses the road. The next section of the route heads right immediately after this bridge, but today's walk ends here.

A calm day on the harbour at Barmouth

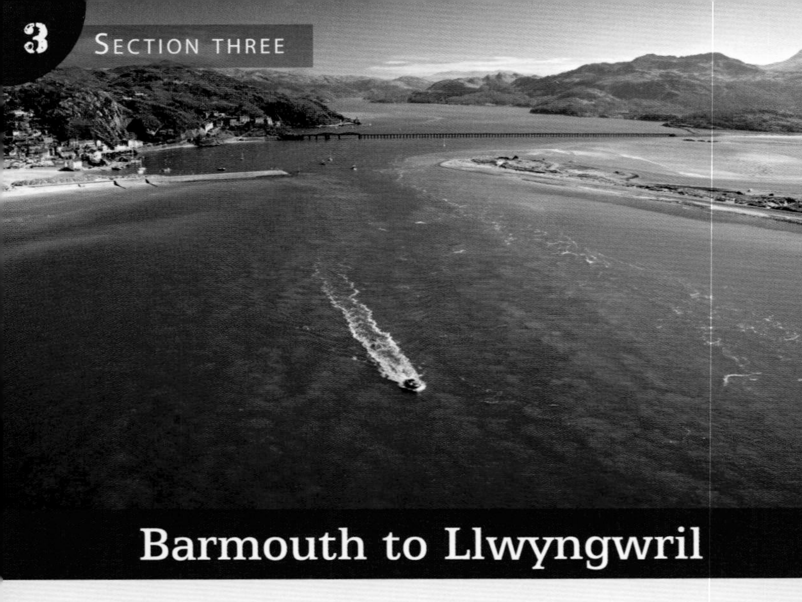

Barmouth to Llwyngwril

Distance: *14 kilometres / 8 miles* | **Start:** *Barmouth Harbour SH 615 154* | **Finish:** *St Celynnin's Church, Llwyngwril SH 591 093* | **Maps:** *Ordnance Survey Explorer OL23 Cadair Idris & Llyn Tegid, Landranger 124 Porthmadog and Dolgellau*

Outline: A shorter day with lots of variety, including the stunning Mawddach estuary and a high road through an ancient landscape.

The crossing of Barmouth Bridge provides a spectacular start to day three of this section of the Wales Coast Path. Beyond the river and the salt marsh, the route follows Fairbourne's sea wall before heading inland through a fascinating disused slate quarry. A high lane, with excellent views of the coast, then passes through an area of prehistoric remains before the route drops, via a grassy path and quiet farm tracks, to the coastal village of Llwyngwril.

Services: *Barmouth has a good range of facilities, including accommodation, places to eat, cash machines, shops and public toilets. Fairbourne also has places to stay and to eat, as well as shops (a few hundred metres off route) and public toilets. Llwyngwril has a more limited choice, but its facilities include accommodation, a pub serving food, a small shop and public toilets. As on previous days, this section passes several stations on the Cambrian Coast railway line, providing points at which the route could be cut short. Blue Line Cabs, Barmouth | 07585 855243 | www.bluelinecabsbarmouthtaxi.com*

Don't miss: **Barmouth Bridge** — longest bridge in Wales | **Fairbourne Steam Railway** – narrow-gauge heritage line | **Blue Lake** – flooded quarry pit

▲ *The mouth of the Afon Mawddach at Barmouth*

Barmouth

Barmouth served as a port for many centuries — possibly as early as medieval times. Sixteenth-century exports mentioned in the Welsh Port Books include grain, timber, wool and herrings. Later, slate was added to the list and became an important part of local trade. From the 1760s until the middle of the nineteenth century, shipbuilding was a major employer too, with about 350 ships constructed during this period.

One of the town's oldest buildings is Tŷ Gwyn, which is thought to date back to about 1465. Now home to a museum and café, it may once have been associated with port activities. A more colourful local story claims it was a safe house for meetings of Lancastrian supporters during the Wars of the Roses. It is said that Jasper Tudor — the Earl of Pembroke and the uncle of the future King Henry VII — came here to plot the overthrow of Richard III, the last of the Plantagenet kings.

Another interesting building is the tiny Tŷ Crwn, built in the 1830s to house drunks. Circular in shape — so that the Devil had no corners in which to hide — it was divided in two: one half for women, the other for men. Close to the harbour, it was recently restored and is open to the public.

The sea has played an important role in Barmouth's history

Walking on water: *The Wales Coast Path crosses Barmouth Bridge*

The route: **Barmouth to Llwyngwril**

1 From the point at which the railway crosses the esplanade road, turn right to walk roughly east along the **A496**. Head gently up the hill. You'll soon have a rock face on your left, covered in a wire mesh to prevent rock falls from hitting the road. As soon as the rock face ends, follow the surfaced path to the right of the road. This passes through the toll booth and crosses **Barmouth Bridge** over the beautiful **Mawddach estuary**.

The river cuts through the heart of the mountains: with the gnarly Rhinogs to the north and Cadair Idris to the south. Looking upstream from the middle of Wales's longest bridge, it seems as if you're crossing one of the great rivers of the UK. It's easy to imagine the Afon Mawddach heading inland for many, many miles; in fact, its source is just a few kilometres inland.

Barmouth Bridge is a grade II-listed structure. Built in 1867 for both rail and foot traffic, it consists of a largely wooden viaduct and a swing-bridge section that used to be opened to allow large ships to sail upstream. Up until fairly recently, pedestrians and cyclists had to pay a 90p toll to cross, but the couple who lived in the toll-house — and were paid to collect the payments — left in 2013.

2 Having crossed the water, keep to the path beside the railway until, just before **Morfa Mawddach Station**, you see a small gate to the right. Go through this to cross the railway. A raised path now hugs the southern edge of the salt marsh — with great views back across to Barmouth and the hills rising behind the town.

3 On the far side of the **saltmarsh**, the path reaches a road. Turn left here: either along the road, or, along the path beside the sea wall. If you choose the

Birth of the National Trust

The gorse and bracken-covered hillside immediately above Barmouth is Dinas Oleu. Given to the National Trust by Fanny Talbot in 1895 — its inaugural year — this was the first parcel of land ever donated to what is now one of Europe's largest conservation charities. Mrs Talbot was a friend of Octavia Hill, one of the three co-founders of the National Trust along with Canon Hardwicke Rawnsley and Sir Robert Hunter.

latter, watch carefully for the point at which the road — and the toy railway running alongside it — swings left. This is about 900 metres after the Wales Coast Path joins it. If you wish to make use of the facilities in **Fairbourne**, including shops, public toilets, the railway station and the start of the miniature railway, you'll need to follow this road round to the left.

Wales is home to a number of narrow-gauge heritage railways, several of which are passed as you walk the Snowdonia and Ceredigion Coast stretch of the Wales Coast Path. Most were built to service local industries and only later became tourist attractions, but the one at Fairbourne served tourists almost from day one. It started out as a two-foot gauge, horse-drawn tramway in 1895, originally used to transport construction materials for the building of the village. It was converted to a 15-inch gauge steam line in 1916.

Those wishing to continue on the Coast Path should keep to the surfaced path at the back of the beach. This continues for one kilometre beyond the point at which the road heads away from the sea. It ends just after a yellow emergency phone.

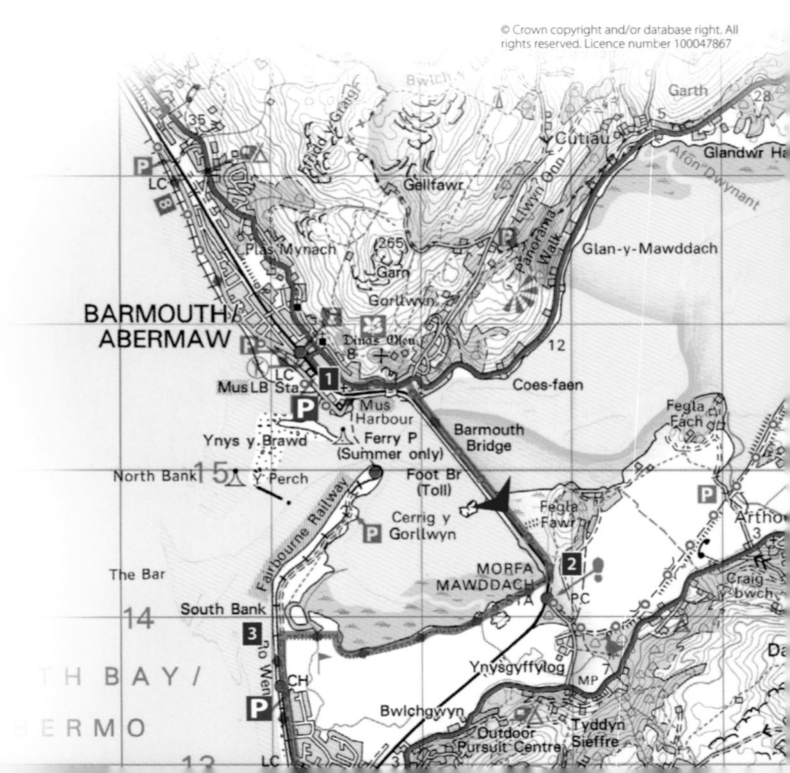

Seaside trip: *Fairbourne Steam Railway started life a horse-drawn tramway*

There are a number of tank traps on Fairbourne's beach. Also known as 'dragon's teeth', these large concrete posts were placed here during World War Two and were designed to prevent German tanks from moving inland in the event of an invasion by Hitler's forces.

4 Drop down the steps here and follow the road inland, under the **railway** and up to the **A493**. Turn left and walk along the pavement beside the main road for about 450 metres, taking the next lane on the right. Follow this dead-end lane, as it climbs steadily, for about 500 metres and then go through a gate on the right.

5 A quarry track heads uphill through the trees, soon swinging right. This zig-zags its way up the hillside. At the edge of the quarry, you reach a fork. Bear left here, heading uphill again. The route then swings left — through a gate.

For those interested in industrial archaeology — or taking a cooling dip in the Blue Lake — it's worth devoting a bit of time to exploring the disused **Goleuwern Slate Quarry**. *The Blue Lake itself, located in an old quarry pit and surrounded by sheer walls, can only be reached via a low-roofed tunnel. But that doesn't put off the many families who swim here on hot summer days.*

Soon after passing under power lines, take a narrower path dropping to the left. (This turning is easy to miss.) The path goes through a gate and swings right as it passes through the trees and then bracken. A stream soon has to be forded: a tricky undertaking after heavy rain. Beyond the metal gate on the other side, the path continues through bracken. Bear right at a faint fork to pass to the right of a tiny ruined building, and then head uphill beside a **small stream**. This too has to be forded, although this shouldn't present any difficulties. After a gap in a wall, keep straight on, ignoring a trail to the right. Walk with a wall on your left and then pass to the left of a small outbuilding. A short section of walled track soon swings right — down towards the isolated house at **Cyfannedd-fawr**. Follow the vehicle track away from the building, soon reaching a minor road.

Far-reaching: *Looking back across the Mawddach estuary towards the Llŷn peninsula*

6 Turn right along the asphalt. This high lane is followed for 2.8 kilometres, climbing from the forest to enjoy spectacular views out to sea and across to the Llŷn peninsula.

You'll pass several standing stones along the way as well as an ancient settlement, clearly visible to the right of the road. According to local stories, the stones are the result of fights between the lowland giant Gwril and his cousin, the mountain giant, Idris. The pair used to hurl rocks at each other.

7 Eventually, with a pond just below, the road swings right. Leave it here by bearing left along a broad, grassy path beside the wall on the left. This delightful route provides easy walking, keeping more or less to the 200-metre contour; don't be tempted by any other paths heading up to the left. Eventually, after a gate, it begins a slow descent towards **Llwyngwril**. On joining a surfaced lane, simply keep heading downhill in the same direction. You drop into Llwyngwril at a junction with the main road through the village. Turn left and walk beside the road as far as **St Celynnin's Church** at the southern end of the village. Today's section ends at the church.

Llwyngwril to Aberdyfi

Distance: *19 kilometres / 12 miles* | **Start:** *St Celynnin's Church, Llwyngwril SH 591 093* | **Finish:** *Tourist Information Centre, Aberdyfi SN 614 959* | **Maps:** *Ordnance Survey Explorer OL23 Cadair Idris & Llyn Tegid, Landrangers 124 Porthmadog and Dolgellau, and 135 Aberystwyth and Machynlleth*

Outline: A varied day that starts by crossing an ancient, farmed landscape before taking to country lanes and ending with a long beach walk.

The Wales Coast Path heads inland briefly today as it takes to worn trackways and trails that pass through centuries-old enclosures with some excellent views out to sea. Prehistoric remains dot the landscape, including an Iron Age hill fort just above Llwyngwril at the start of the walk. Dropping back to sea level, the route heads across farmland and along quiet lanes to reach the town of Tywyn. Finally, it ends with another long, sandy beach backed by dunes leading all the way to the Dyfi estuary.

Services: *Llwyngwril is only a small village, but it does have accommodation, a pub serving food, a small shop and public toilets. Further south, both Tywyn and Aberdyfi are larger settlements with a broader range of facilities, including cash machines and, at Tywyn, a decent-sized supermarket. (Aberdyfi Tourist Information Centre, Wharf Gardens, Sea View Terrace | 01654 767321 | tic.aberdyfi@eryri-npa.org.uk). As on previous days, this section passes several stations on the Cambrian Coast railway line, providing points at which the route could be cut short. Dyfi Cabs, Aberdyfi | 07831 551538*

Don't miss: **Castell y Gaer** – Iron Age fort | **Pont Tonfanau** – impressive bowspring bridge | **Talyllyn Railway** – world's first preserved railway

▲ *Looking northwards up the beach from the mouth of the Afon Dyfi*

Llwyngwril

Llwyngwril is a pleasant little village sitting astride both the A493 and the Afon Gwril, which comes rushing down from the hills at the western end of the Cadair Idris massif. Water from the river was once harnessed to power a number of mills in the area, and even provided electricity for the village.

The settlement has strong links with the early Quaker movement. The celebrated preacher George Fox visited nearby Dolgellau in 1657, spreading his ideas about a new type of Christianity that eschewed rituals and believed in equality. Among his most prominent local followers were the Humphrey family, who lived at Llwyn Du, Llwyngwril. In about 1664, they gifted a plot of their land for use as a burial ground for Quakers. Known as Bryn Tallwyn, it still exists today.

The Quakers were persecuted during the seventeenth century — some, including Owen Humphrey, imprisoned for their radical beliefs. When, in 1681, William Penn set up a Quaker community in what is now Pennsylvania, many followed him across the Atlantic. The Humphreys were among those who fled to the New World, and helped Penn establish his community there.

A stream flows into the sea at Llwyngwril

The route: Llwyngwril to Aberdyfi

1 Take the narrow lane heading steeply uphill between **St Celynnin's Church** and a small cemetery. After crossing a cattle grid and then passing a small building to the left of the road, you'll see the gorse-topped remains of **Castell y Gaer**, an Iron Age fort. Continue uphill on the road.

2 Immediately after a second cattle grid, turn right along a concrete farm track — towards the farm buildings at **Carn-gadell-uchaf**. Head to the higher track where a rough route drops to a **large farm shed**. When the track swings left to reach the **farmhouse**, keep straight ahead and go through a small gate. Drop to cross a **stream**, followed quickly by a wooden stile.

The paths are generally unclear on the ground as you make your way across the farmland, so you'll need to pay close attention to the map and walk description. This next section can be lovely in sunny weather, with some great views and a wonderful sense of timelessness: where ancient routeways cross a landscape that has been farmed in much the same way for many, many generations. In wet weather though, when the ground is muddy, it's quite a different experience.

Climb the short slope and turn sharp right to head down the side

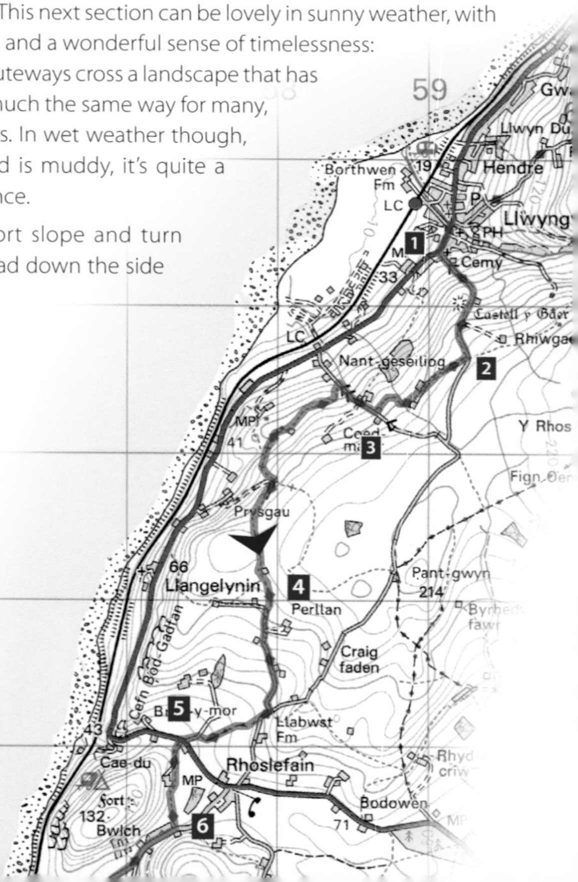

Seascape: *There are panoramic views as the coast path climbs high above Llwyngwril*

of the field. After about 100 metres, swing away from the wooded ravine to pass through two wall gaps. After the second one, stay high — walking along a faint, grassy track with a fence on your left. After the next stile, continue in the same direction, heading downhill beside a wall. Cross the stile at the bottom to reach a surfaced lane.

3 Turn right and follow the lane downhill for about 300 metres. Watch for a set of steps on the left. These lead up to a stile. Having climbed this, head left to walk up the slope, gradually making your way towards the fence on the right. Ford a small stream before crossing a stile in the fence. Head uphill beside the fence and go through a small gate in the top wall.

Turn right to walk with the wall on your right. After a gap in an intervening wall, a faint trail comes away from the field boundary on the right. It passes through another wall gap and then continues to a ladder stile close to a ruined cottage. Pass to the left of the abandoned building and immediately climb to the large gate to the right.

Once through this, bear left along a faint, rising track. Keep to the top of the embankment and then make your way round to the right of a particularly dense stand of gorse. Once round it, swing back to the left to drop to a gap in a tumbledown old wall. Turn left and go through a large gate. Take the path

Cae-du
Rhoslefain
MP
Fort
132
Bwlch
6
Bodowen
71
Llanfendigaid
28
Fort
Castell
Waenfach
Clos-bach
Bronclydwr
Nantycynog
69
Tonfanau
Cefncamberth
178
Beacon
Tal-y-gareg
Earthwork
28
7
Quarry (dis)
Tal-y-gareg
Fort
Pen-y-wern
Pant
41
Domen Ddreiniog
Aber Dysynni
Bryn
Crynllwyn
Broad Water
Morfa Gwyllt
Ynysymaengwyn
Sluice
Wks
Morfa Camp (Barracks)
82
7
Croes-faen
Pall Mall
8
Cemy
Hen-dy
Bryn-y-mor
Pendre
LC
Ty-mawr
P
57
Groynes
Sch
Hospl
TYWYN
Pantyneuadd
Mus
Bron-prys
198
PC
25
60
172
Neptune Hall
Penllyn
Escuan Hall
MS
Bod Talog
Escuan Isaf
11
LC
5
Caethle Fm
Rhowniar
MP
5
Llwybr Arfordir
Wales Coast
A 493
Ffridd Cefn

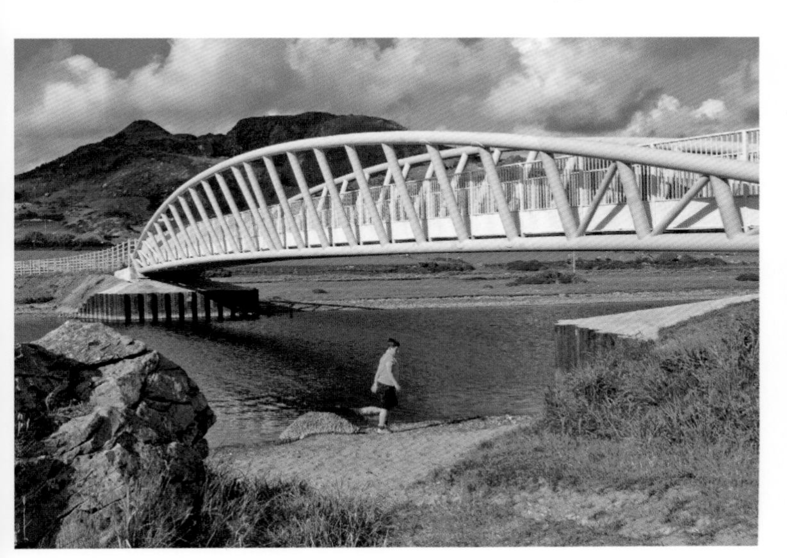

Graceful arch: *The Pont Tonfanau was installed in 2013*

slanting up to the right. Once through the gate at the top, cross a muddy track to continue uphill with a wall on your right. Beyond the next gate, turn right. You soon walk with a fence on your right. In the next field, you will see two trails heading left. Take the one further right — the less clear option. It heads up to and through a gate. The route continues uphill — to the right of what looks like the remains an old, grass-covered wall. Once through the next gate, walk with the field boundary on your right for a few metres. Then, when it bends right, keep straight ahead — through a shallow dip in the field.

Beyond the ladder stile, pass to the left of a narrow stand of young trees. Turn right through a gate on the other side of a small ruined building. Almost immediately, go through a second metal gate on the left. Walk straight across the next field on a very faint path.

4 After going through the gate in the field corner, head downhill on a rough track. Cross the stile next to a cattle grid and then, ignoring the track to the left, continue downhill. The rough track later goes over to asphalt. Follow this downhill for 600 metres. About 120 metres after a sharp bend to the right, leave the lane by turning right along a broad, grassy track between hedgerows. You lose the hedge on the right beyond the first gate, but the partially sunken track continues downhill. Turn left when you come out on to a surfaced lane and follow this down to the **A493** on the edge of **Rhoslefain**.

Inland sea?: *The Afon Dysynni widens into Broad Water, near Tywyn*

5 Cross the main road to pick up a track to the right of the solitary house opposite. Follow this uphill for about 130 metres and then go through a metal farm gate on the left. Now keep close to the field boundary on your right. Go through a large gate to the left of the farm buildings at **Bron-y-foel** and continue parallel with the field boundary on your right. Beyond the next gate, aim to the left of the large rock outcrop and then go through a small gate directly below a white-washed house. Make your way up to the building.

6 Turn right along the quiet road in front of the white-washed house. Ignoring a private lane to the left early on, follow this road for almost 2.5 kilometres to **Tonfanau.**

Tonfanau isn't a village as such: more a scattering of farms and isolated houses. The population is tiny, but in the 1970s, its ranks were swelled by a sudden and brief influx of Ugandan Asians fleeing from Idi Amin. In August 1972, Amin, then president of Uganda, gave the country's Asian population 90 days to leave. The UK ended up taking more than 27,000 refugees, setting up 12 resettlement camps nationwide. More than 1,000 were taken to the former army camp at Tonfanau, which had been used during World War Two as an anti-aircraft training facility. The refugees stayed for about six months, later being dispersed around the country. Little remains of the camp today, although some of its buildings and old roadways are used for motorbike racing events.

7 About 400 metres after passing **Tonfanau Station**, take the sealed path on the right, the start of which has bollards across it. (This is opposite the entrance to **Cefncamberth**.) Turn left in a short while and follow the broad track to the new footbridge (Pont Tonfanau) over **Afon Dysynni**. Having crossed, keep straight ahead — along the quiet road that is used, it seems, only by dog-walkers, Wales Coast Path hikers and tankers accessing the water treatment works.

Just inland is the tidal lagoon of **Broad Water.** *There used to be a small ship-building yard here. Today, it's a Site of Special Scientific Interest, and is popular with bird-watchers. Among the species that can be seen are coots, cormorants, grebes, moorhens and red-breasted merganser.*

8 Soon after reaching the edge of **Tywyn**, you come to a T-junction. Turn right here, quickly going over the level crossing. Follow this lane until it ends and then drop down to the path beside the sea wall. Turn left and follow

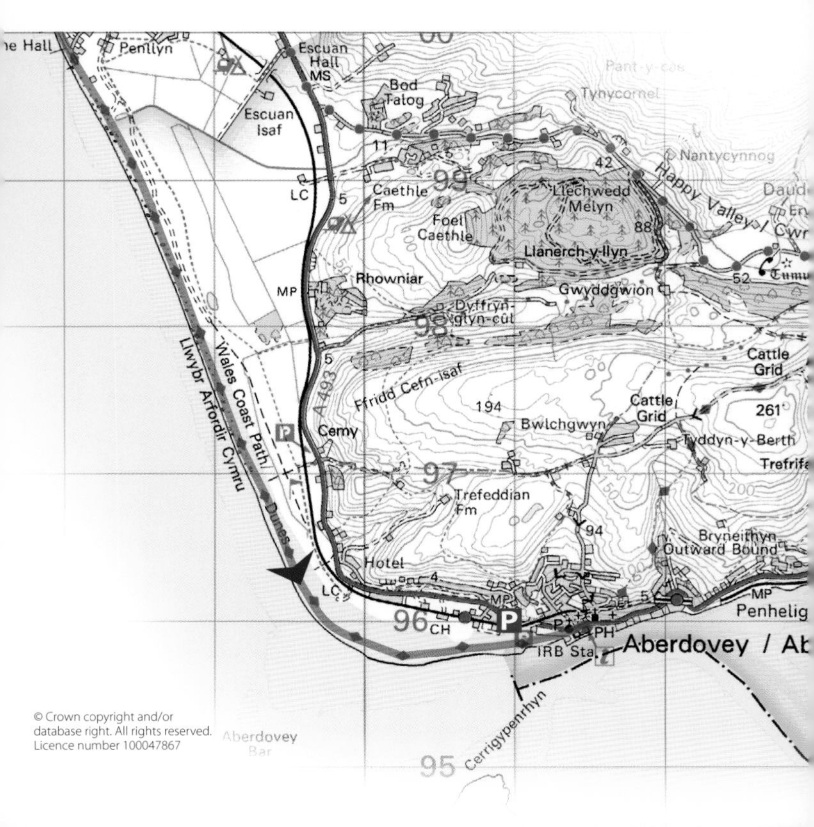

Blue and white: *Cardigan Bay seem from high above the Dyfi estuary*

this to the main seafront car park in **Tywyn**. Those wishing to end the day in **Tywyn** should turn left here and follow the road under the railway bridge and up into the main part of town.

For those heading into Tywyn, there are two must-see attractions: the Talyllyn Railway (see panel) and the Cadfan Stone, housed in St Cadfan's Church.

Thought to date from the ninth century, the inscription on this two-metre high pillar is the earliest known example of written Welsh. The church, located next to the town's tiny cinema, is also home to two medieval effigies and the healing well that first drew St Cadfan and his monks to settle here.

The coast path, however, continues along the seafront. You can either use the pavement to the left of the car park and regain the sea wall later, or you can follow the pedestrian route round to the right of the car park — not recommended when the sea is particularly rough. Follow the sea wall to the southern end of Tywyn, past a caravan site, and then join a clear path at the back of the beach. You are later able to drop on to the beach proper. The small dunes at the back of the beach soon give way to a mess of pebbles before walkers encounter a more significant dune system.

In total, it's almost 6 kilometres from the edge of the last caravan site at Tywyn to Aberdyfi — a lovely, calming walk in a gentle breeze, but considerably more challenging when you've got strong winds coming in off the sea. Leave the beach close to the **RNLI Lifeboat Station** slipway in **Aberdyfi** and turn right along the road. The **Tourist Information Centre**, where today's walk ends, is set back on the right, just after the toilet block in a few metres.

Talyllyn Railway

This 12-kilometre, narrow-gauge line bills itself as the world's first preserved railway. It was built in the mid-1860s to serve the Bryn Eglwys slate quarry. The line runs from Tywyn to Nant Gwernol, from where horse-drawn tramways used to continue higher into the hills. After the quarry's closure in 1947, it seemed the line would be lost, but a group of enthusiasts stepped in and have kept it running ever since. For more details, see: www.talyllyn.co.uk.

Aberdyfi to Machynlleth

Distance: *12 miles/19 kilometres* | **Start:** *Tourist Information Centre, Aberdyfi SN 614 959* | **Finish:** *Clock tower at junction of A487 and A489 in Machynlleth SH 745 007* | **Maps:** *Ordnance Survey Explorer OL23 Cadair Idris & Llyn Tegid, Landranger 135 Aberystwyth and Machynlleth*

Outline: A lovely day high above the Afon Dyfi with great hill views — only briefly dropping into the valley to pass through Pennal.

Abandoning the coast again, the day starts with a steep climb from Aberdyfi to gain the superb Panorama Walk. Striding out on a spur of high ground between Happy Valley and the Afon Dyfi, you're able to enjoy great hill views. The route drops briefly to farmland and woodland before climbing again, from the village of Pennal, to flirt with the southern edge of the vast Dyfi Forest. A short section of road walking follows, ending in historic Machynlleth.

Services: *Aberdyfi isn't a huge settlement, but it does have accommodation, several places to eat, some small shops and public toilets. (Aberdyfi Tourist Information Centre, Wharf Gardens, Sea View Terrace | 01654 767321 | tic.aberdyfi@eryri-npa.org.uk). Pennal has a pub and public toilets. Machynlleth is the largest settlement since Porthmadog and, as such, has a wide range of facilities including accommodation, places to eat, cash machines, shops and public toilets. Peter's Taxi, Machynlleth | 07969 997039*

Don't miss: **Panorama Walk** – extensive views | **Carn March Arthur** – site associated with King Arthur | **Cefn Caer** – medieval hall house

▲ *The Afon Dyfi forms the border between Gwynedd and Ceredigion*

Aberdyfi

Aberdyfi has a gentler, more laid-back feel to it than Barmouth. Although its origins are similar and it's now also a popular holiday resort, it has managed to avoid much of the tackiness associated with its neighbour to the north. Wander the streets and alleyways winding up the hillside to get a feel for the place and enjoy some great views out to sea and across the Dyfi estuary.

The town was at its peak in the eighteenth and nineteenth centuries when slate and bark were being exported from here. Penhelig, the name given to the eastern side of the town, was home to seven shipyards where several dozen ships were constructed in the middle of the nineteenth century.

The town is closely associated with the Atlantis-style legend of the lost kingdom of Cantre'r Gwaelod, said to lie beneath the waters of Cardigan Bay. It is claimed that, as you walk the beach at Aberdyfi, you can sometimes hear the church bells of Cantre'r Gwaelod's drowned church. A folk song, *Clychau Aberdyfi* or *The Bells of Aberdovey*, popularised the myth in the eighteenth century.

In 1941, the first ever Outward Bound centre was opened in Aberdyfi, leading to what is now the largest provider of bursary-assisted outdoor education in the UK.

Colourful waterfront buildings at Aberdyfi

The route: **Aberdyfi to Machynlleth**

1 With your back to the **Tourist Information Centre** in **Aberdyfi**, turn right along the main road. As the pavement ends, soon after you draw level with the **Literary Institute** building, you'll see a sloping high wall to the left of the road. This hides a flight of steps — and the next section of the Wales Coast Path — which can be accessed from the far (lower) end of the wall. On reaching a surfaced lane, cross diagonally right to climb the next set of steps — beside **Aberdovey Hillside Village**. There are good views down to the town as you gain height. Where the path swings sharp right, keep straight ahead beside the wall on your left at first. A clear path then winds its way up the hillside between stands of gorse and through a gate. *Look behind for a view out across the Dyfi estuary to Borth: 7 kilometres away as the crow flies, but 43 kilometres, or a full two days' walking, via the Coast Path.*

Ignoring a path to the left, climb to a wooden stile. Once over this, pass to the left of the stables and caravan, and then swing half-right — making sure you stay on level ground as you aim for a clear but narrow path through the gorse. A pleasant path now hugs the hillside above a wooded ravine. The gap between the path

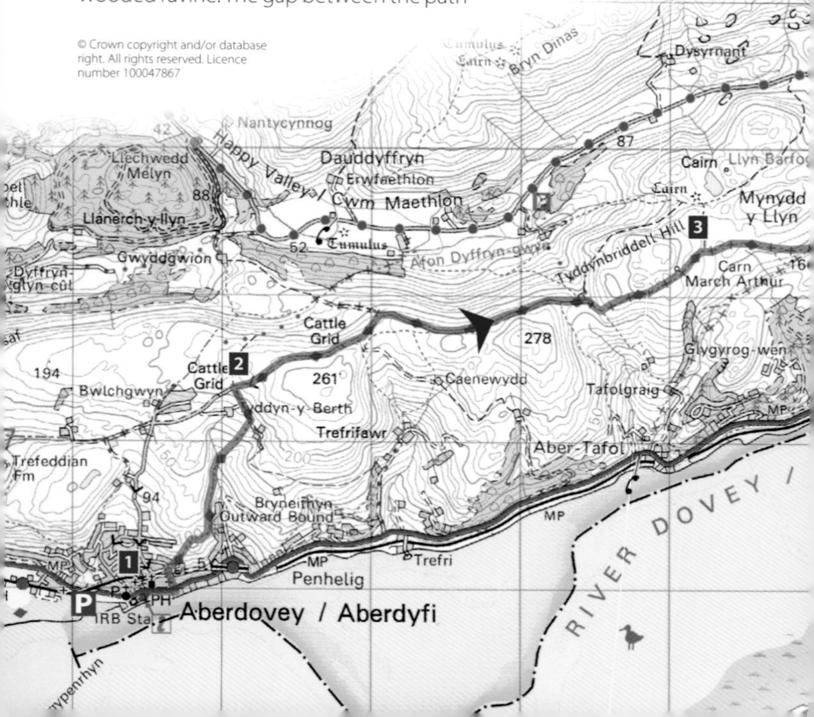

Joyful sight: *The gently rolling countryside around Cwm Maethlon, or Happy Valley*

and the stream in the ravine is gradually closed until, as you go through a small gate, you are standing right next to it. Cross the stile ahead and then, a few metres further on, cross the tiny bridge.

Turn right after the next stile but then, almost immediately, swing left at the top of the short slope. Climbing steadily, the route, indistinct on the ground, passes through a gap in a line of small trees. Continuing uphill, aim slightly left of the large farm sheds at **Erw-pistyll**. A set of gates about 100 metres to the left of the buildings provides access to a farm track, along which you turn left.

2 On reaching a narrow lane, turn right — still climbing for a little while longer, but more gently now. From the top of the rise, you are able to look across to the rolling hills north of Cwm Maethlon, also known as **Happy Valley**. This lovely scene accompanies you for the next 2.5 kilometres — until the asphalt ends at **Bwlch Farm**. Go through the gates here and then follow a clear track (known as the **Panorama Walk**) beyond the isolated farmhouse. This swings right to cross to the other side of the ridge: the view of Happy Valley now being replaced by the Dyfi estuary to the south and the low-lying hills beyond. Before long, the views ahead open out again with rolling hills stretching far into the distance.

Heading inland: *Hikers on the aptly-named Panorama Walk*

You are now walking with a wall on your right. Where this becomes a fence, look to the left of the track and you will see a stone marker called **Carn March Arthur**, or the Stone of Arthur's Horse.

3 About 200 metres beyond Stone March Arthur, keep right at a clear fork. The track eventually begins dropping away from the high ground, later skirting the edge of a conifer plantation. It comes out on to a farm lane close to **Cefn-cynhafal.** Turn right and follow this quiet road all the way down to the **A493**.

4 Just short of the main road, take the pedestrian route to the right. Carefully cross the road diagonally left to pick up a clear track. This quickly bends right. When it does so, you will see two gates to the left of the bend. Go through the left-hand of these to access another track. This too quickly bends right and, as it does so, go through the gate on the left. Follow a less obvious track for about 180 metres beyond the gate and then, as it swings left, branch off right to pick up a broad path along the base of a lightly wooded slope. Beyond a metal kissing-gate, head straight across the field towards a **foot-bridge**. Cross and walk up to the top left-hand corner of this narrow field.

5 Beyond the kissing-gate, then turn left along the quiet lane. Almost immediately, turn sharp right — almost back on yourself — along the driveway of **Penmaendyfi**. Follow this round to the left and then walk straight between the buildings to a farm gate. Once through this, bear half-left up the field, aiming for a wooden power pole with a waymarker on it. Continue uphill in roughly the same direction to reach a metal kissing-gate. Beyond this, a trail leads through an area of mature woodland.

Arthur's horse's stone?

Close to the path is Carn March Arthur. Let your imagination take over, and the indentation in the rock starts to looks like it's been made by a horse's hoof — the horse of King Arthur. Local legend has it that Arthur came here to kill a monster, the avanc, which lived in nearby Llyn Barfog. He threw an enormous chain around the monster and, with the help of his horse, dragged it from the lake and killed it.

All alone: *An isolated cottage close to the slopes of Tarranhendre*

After two more gates, you enter thicker woodland on the edge of the **Plas Talgarth** holiday resort. Almost immediately, descend the steps on the right and turn sharp right along a well-constructed trail that drops to a level path. Turn left along this. Pass to the right of the first chalet, go through the gap in the wall on the left and then follow the **surfaced driveway** down to the right. Passing the last few chalets on your right, turn left at a T-junction and follow this lane to the **A493**.

The mansion at Plas Talgarth was built by Humphrey Edwards during the eighteenth century. It later passed, through marriage, to the Thruston family and is now part of a holiday and leisure complex.

The village of Pennal is close to the site of a Roman fort called Cefn Caer. Little remains of the five-acre site today other than some earthworks. It is believed the fort may have been occupied in the middle of the first century. It probably guarded a crossing on the Afon Dyfi, part of the Sarn Helen Roman road which linked Aberconwy in the north with Carmarthen, 260 kilometres away.

A medieval hall house now stands at Cefn Caer, and it is reputed that Owain Glyndŵr established his base here while he set up his Welsh Parliament at nearby Machynlleth. It may have been while he was staying here in 1406 that he wrote the Pennal Letter to King Charles VI of France, asking for his military assistance to fight the English and setting out his vision of an independent Wales.

6 Turn right along the main road. After passing the **school** on the edge of **Pennal**, the road crosses a bridge. Turn left immediately after this. Having climbed beyond the village, ignore a road and a track to the left.

7 About 1.2 kilometres after leaving the A493, bear right along a broad forest track. Bear right at an obvious fork, soon passing and ignoring another track heading up to the right. The track climbs slowly and steadily through the forest. The tree cover is not too thick, and you're able to enjoy some great views across to Tarranhendre to the left. Soon after a sweeping bend, about 2 kilometres into the forest, ignore a track dropping to the left: our way continues uphill. Bear left as another broad forest track comes in from the right.

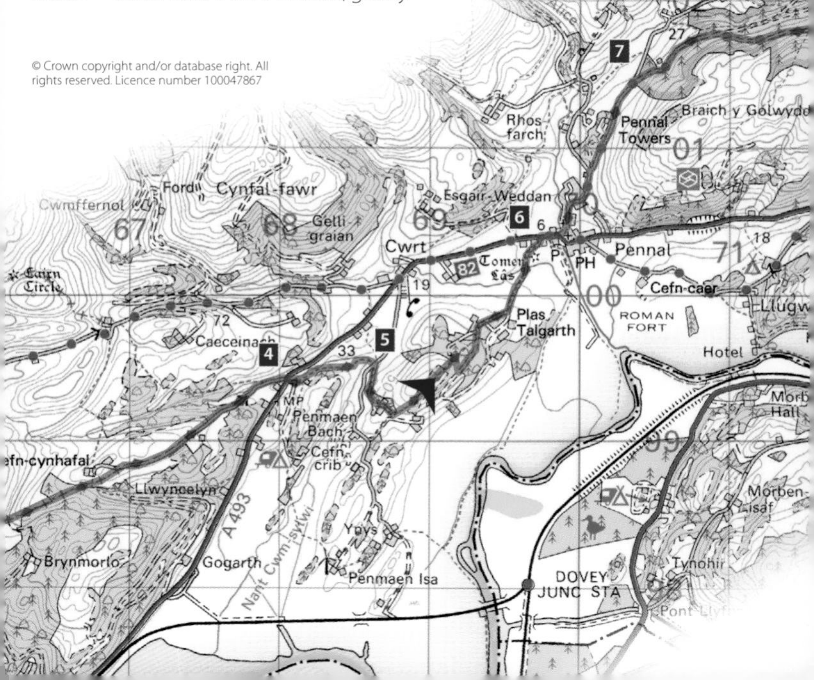

8 Finally, having followed forest tracks for about 3.2 kilometres, take a narrow path heading up to the right. (This comes soon after you begin climbing out of a small dip in the track.) The path climbs through an area of saplings — a cruelly steep ascent at this stage of what has already been a fairly tough day. With a grand hilly outlook to the east, you reach a stile at the forest fence. Cross this and keep straight ahead — beside the fence on your right at first. When the fence kinks right, the route — little more than a narrow, grassy trail — comes away from it. But don't stray too far from the fence and the trees on your right; there are trails heading off to the left, but these are red herrings. Simply head downhill — roughly east — and you will eventually draw level with the fence on the right again.

9 Go through a farm gate and then turn right along the surfaced lane. After about 1km, this lane drops you back on to the **A493**.

As the Coast Path drops back to the A493, it passes close to Bron-yr-aur. A rather unassuming eighteenth-century cottage, this building figures highly in the history of rock music because of its close associations with Led Zeppelin. In 1970, vocalist Robert Plant and guitarist Jimmy Page stayed here for a while writing songs for the band's third album Led Zeppelin III. These included Bron-Y-Aur Stomp, which celebrates the Gwynedd countryside and Plant's dog Strider, and the instrumental Bron-Yr-Aur, which appeared on the Physical Graffiti album in 1975. Not surprisingly, the cottage has become a site of pilgrimage for fans of the legendary band.

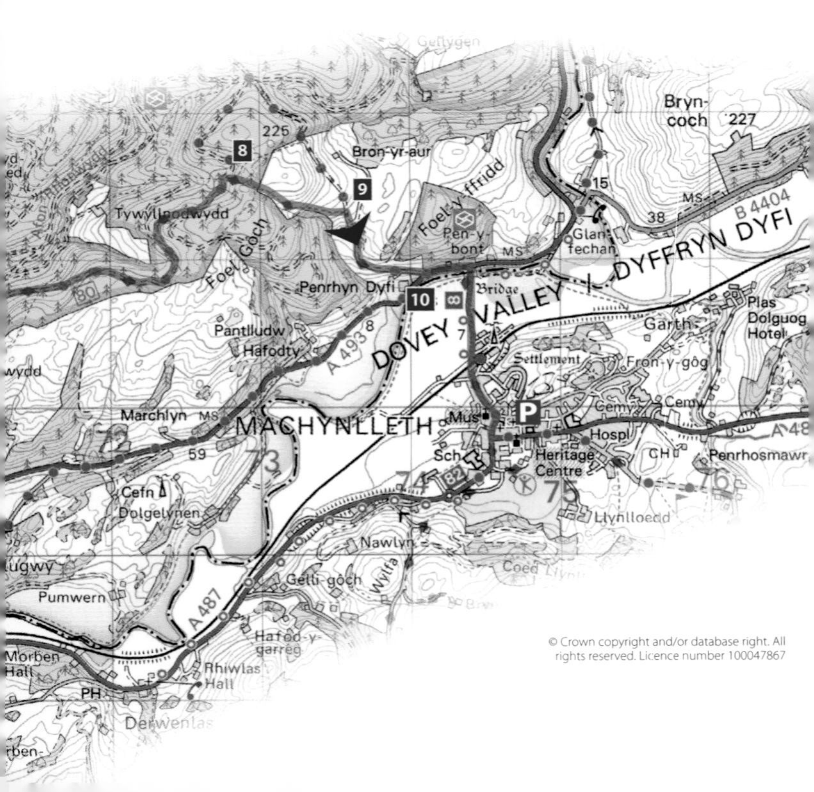

Ancient crossing: *The bridge over the Afon Dyfi near Machynlleth*

10 Turn left along the main road, keeping in very close to the side of the asphalt as there is no pavement or grass verge. Turn right at the T-junction to cross the **Pont Dyfi** on the **A487** — crossing the county border from Gwynedd to Powys and leaving the Snowdonia National Park as you do so. On the other side of the river, you pick up a shared cycleway and pedestrian path that leads as far as the **railway bridge** — and **station** — on the edge of **Machynlleth**. Continue along the road, passing under the railway and follow it into the centre of the town. Today's section ends at the prominent **clock tower** opposite the junction with the A489.

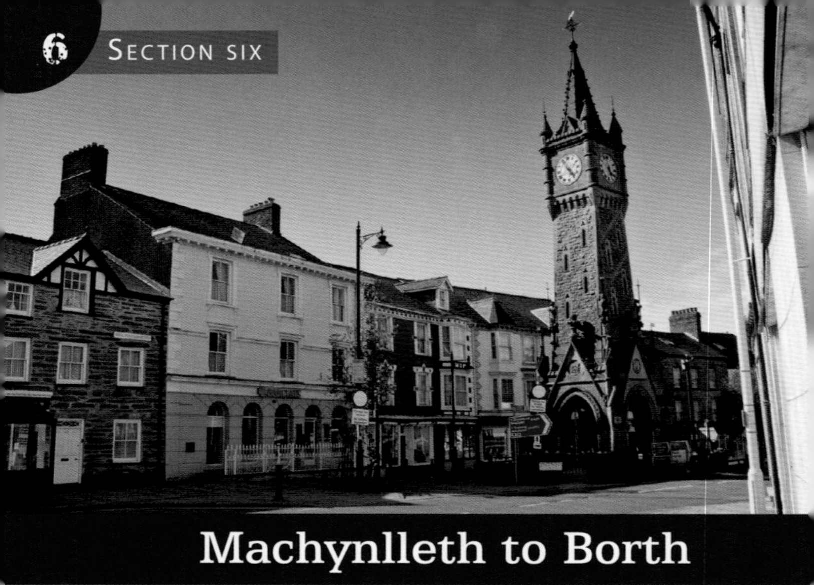

Machynlleth to Borth

Distance: *24 kilometres / 15 miles (or 29 kilometres / 18 miles)* | **Start:** *Clock tower at junction of A487 and A489 in Machynlleth SH 745 007* | **Finish:** *RNLI lifeboat station in Borth SN 608 889 (or Dyfi-Ynyslas National Nature Reserve visitor centre at Ynyslas SN 609 941)* | **Maps:** *Ordnance Survey Explorer OL23 Cadair Idris & Llyn Tegid, and 213 Aberystwyth & Cwm Rheidol, Landranger 135 Aberystwyth and Machynlleth*

Outline: **A long day returning to the coast via gorgeous wooded valleys, forest, open hillsides and the edge of wildlife-rich marshland.**

Leaving Machynlleth, walkers set out on a roller-coaster section of the Wales Coast Path: in and out of wooded valleys, and across farmland with views of hills and coast. After crossing the A487, the walk changes again: now it heads out along the southern edge of the immense marshland of Cors Fochno to the sea at Borth. The Wales Coast Path heads south from here, but those wanting to do all of the Ceredigion Coast Path will first head north to Ynyslas.

Services: *Machynlleth has a wide range of facilities including accommodation, places to eat, cash machines, shops and public toilets. (Aberdyfi Tourist Information Centre, Wharf Gardens, Sea View Terrace | 01654 767321| tic.aberdyfi@eryri-npa.org.uk). B&Bs, pub, café and community shop at Tre'r-ddôl. Borth has places to eat, a cash machine, shops, public toilets and accommodation, including several campsites and a youth hostel. The stretch between Machynlleth and Tre'r-ddôl is never far from the A487, so it is easy to drop down to the main road to find accommodation or catch a bus. Peter's Taxi, Machynlleth | 07969 997039*

Don't miss: **Owain Glyndŵr Centre** – museum and medieval house | **Furnace** – well-preserved iron furnace | **Cors Fochno** – National Nature Reserve

▲ *The famous clock tower in Machynlleth*

Machynlleth

Because of its associations with Owain Glyndŵr, the town of Machynlleth lays claim to the title of 'ancient capital of Wales'. The Welsh leader is said to have had his parliament here in 1404 — possibly on the site of the medieval building on Heol Maengwyn that now houses the Owain Glyndŵr Centre. Home to an interactive exhibition that explains all about Glyndŵr, this free museum is open to the public from Easter until the end of September.

Most of the buildings in the town today were constructed during the nineteenth century, but the Parliament House isn't the only structure in Machynlleth that predates the Victorians: the Royal House, for example, probably dates from the sixteenth century. This merchant's home gets its name from the local story that Charles I stayed here in the 1640s.

The town's most famous structure is, undoubtedly, its prominent clock tower. This was built by public subscription in 1874 to celebrate the 21st birthday of Viscount Castlereagh, whose parents lived at Plas Machynlleth. The seventh Marquess of Londonderry gifted Plas Machynlleth, formerly known as Greenfields, and its grounds to the local council in the middle of the twentieth century.

Owain Glyndŵr's parliament house in Machynlleth is now a museum

The route: **Machynlleth to Borth**

1 From the tall clock tower in the centre of **Machynlleth**, walk south along the **A487**. On the edge of the town, you will see a roundabout ahead. Just before this, the high wall to the left of the road ends. Go sharp left here, over the driveway and through a kissing-gate close to a small **gatehouse**.

The steps leading uphill here are known locally as the **Roman Steps**. *Beyond the first few steps, which are relatively modern, it's clear this rock-hewn stairway is ancient, but there is considerable doubt surrounding its supposed Roman origins.*

When the steps end, continue uphill. Go straight over a track close to a cottage, and then turn left on reaching a minor road, heading uphill at first. Since leaving Machynlleth, the Wales Coast Path has coincided with **Glyndŵr's Way**, a 217-kilometre (135-mile) National Trail that runs from Welshpool to Knighton. Just beyond the brow of the hill though, Glyndŵr's Way heads off to the left, while the Wales Coast Path continues on the road.

2 Having walked along the asphalt for just over 1 kilometre, go through a gate on the right and head straight down the field. Beyond the stile at the bottom of the slope, turn right along the road and then left at a T-junction. At a left bend, take the lane on the right — effectively straight on. Shortly after passing **Garthowen Farm**, step up on to a woodland path to the right of the asphalt. This runs parallel with the road at first. Just after joining another path from the right, the route goes through a farm gate. Walk with the fence on your left and, when this ends, continue in the same direction, soon with a tumbledown wall on your left.

3 Go through a large metal gate on your right and head downhill on the broad forest track. Keep straight ahead, ignoring a

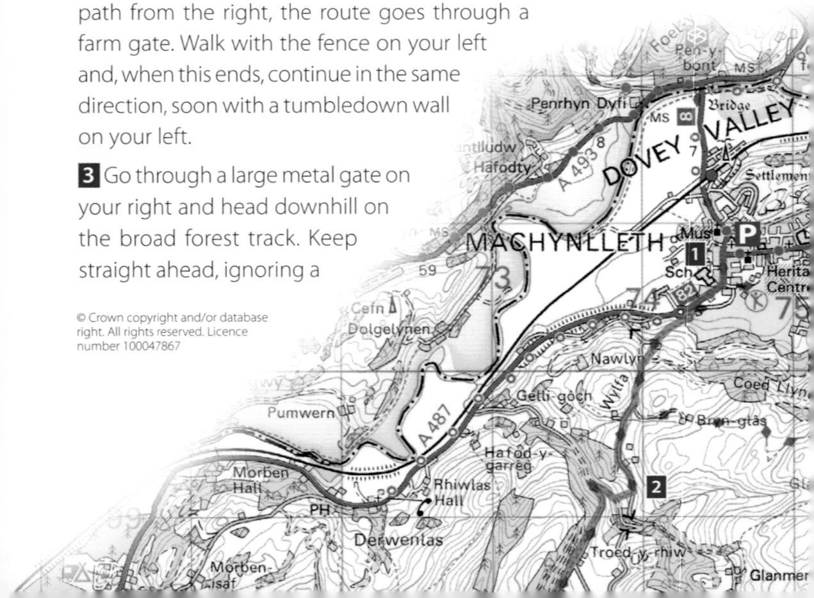

Unspoilt habitat: *Brackish pools and salt marsh on Ynys-hir RSPB reserve*

couple of turnings to the left, and eventually the track becomes a pleasant woodland path, heading downstream through the **Llyfnant Valley**. The river, with its waterfalls and rapids, makes for a lively companion.

A farm gate marks the western edge of the woods. Once through this, walk beside the fence on the left. A rough track is joined close to an **isolated cottage**. At a junction, turn left. About 180 metres after the track crosses the Llyfnant and passes into Ceredigion, take the lane climbing to the left — almost heading back on yourself.

4 Immediately after passing the cottage at **Caerhedyn**, take the path climbing beyond the gate set back slightly on the right. Ascending steeply, this soon enters an area of woodland. As you gain height and the trees thin out, you are able to look across the Afon Dyfi to yesterday's route. At the top of the rise, you break free of the trees and the path cuts a green swathe through the bracken. After a metal gate, swing left, keeping a narrow stand of conifers on your left. Beyond the next gate, a clear trail leads down through the woods. This drops on to a narrow lane, along which you turn right.

Beyond the next group of farm buildings, you find yourself in another gorgeous, wooded ravine — one of several encountered on today's walk. Follow the lane left to cross the **Afon Melindwr** and a cattle grid.

Tidal layby: *The Dyfi Bends, where ships waited for the incoming tide to carry them upriver*

5 About 80 metres after crossing the river, go through the metal kissing-gate on the left. As the grassy path climbs the bracken-covered hillside, the views out over the **Dyfi estuary**, including the **RSPB's Ynys-hir reserve**, open out again. A rock outcrop to the right of the path provides a good place to rest a while: there is a bench here and a view indicator.

On reaching a lane, go left and then take the track on the right — towards **Felin y Cwm**. Just before the track ends near a cottage, go through a small gate straight ahead. Follow the trail down through the trees to the wide, railed **bridge** over **Afon Einion** in the bottom of the valley known as **Artists' Valley**. Having crossed, follow the path to the right, climbing through the trees on the southern side of the valley.

6 Turn right on reaching a minor road and then, in a few metres, take the clear track on the left. (Alternatively, to cut the day short, carry on down the road to **Furnace**. This is the half-way point on this long day, and it's on an hourly bus route between Aberystwyth and Machynlleth.)

At a crossing of ways, go left, ignoring the track climbing to the right. About 120 metres beyond the crossing, go through a kissing-gate on the right. A narrow path runs alongside the trees and past some **ruined buildings**.

Once through a small gate, you lose any sense of a path on the ground. Bear right: up the slope and under the power lines to reach a fence. Turn left to walk downhill with the fence, and then a wall, on your right. Nearing the bottom of the slope, bear left — away from the wall. Drop into a hollow, climb the other side and then continue in the same direction to reach a **wooden footbridge**. Having crossed, go through the gate and swing slightly right to cross diagonally to a small stream on the other side of the field. Walk

Ynys-hir RSPB reserve

The Ynys-hir nature reserve is a mix of wet grassland, oak woods and salt marsh. It's a great place to see nesting waders such as redshank and lapwing as well as little egret. Birds of prey include red kite, peregrine, buzzard and hen harrier, on the verge of extinction in other parts of the UK. In winter, the reserve is home to white-fronted geese that fly in from Greenland.

downhill with the stream on your left and then cross it via the next **bridge**. Go through the kissing-gate, walk beside the fence on the right and then go through a second kissing-gate (on the right). A faint trail drops down a slope and swings right beside a **tiny stream**. After the next **gated bridge**, turn sharp left to walk along the top edge of the field. At the far end, cross another bridge and go through a kissing-gate. Continue straight on, walking with the fence on your right.

7 On entering the **woods**, follow the trail round to the right — heading downhill. (Don't be tempted by a faint path heading left just after the tiny bridge.) Just after the scant remains of a building in a field to the right, the trail swings left — heading uphill. Cross a broad track diagonally left to continue on a path through the trees. Keep right at an obvious fork, staying on a level path. This ends at a **bridge next to a ford**. Cross and turn right, beside the stream. Follow the fence on your left round to the left and uphill. This fenced route comes out close to a minor road.

8 Cross diagonally right to pick up a broad **forest track** on the other side of a sturdy metal barrier. Where the track ends, a narrower path continues in the same direction. This eventually drops you next to the **A487** on the edge of **Tre'r-ddôl**.

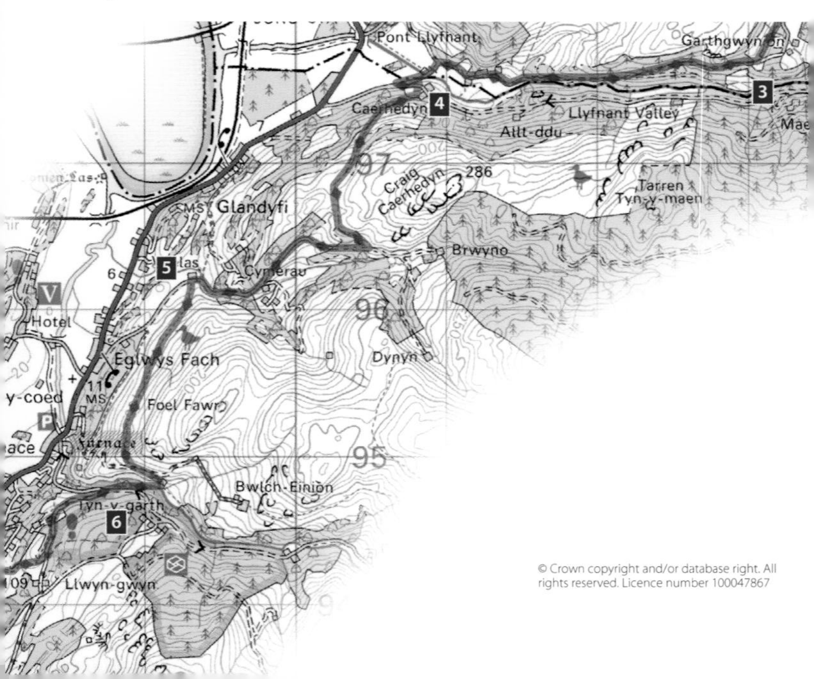

Vantage point: *There are great views north from Foel Fawr*

9 Turn left beside the main road for about 130 metres and take the next lane on the left. Housed in a former petrol station, there is a small **café** and **community shop** on this corner. The lane passes the **Wildfowler pub** and then comes back out on the **A487**. Turn left again to walk beside the main road. There is pavement covering the short distance between here and the next village, which is **Tre Taliesin**.

Lead and copper extraction dominated the village of Tre Taliesin for many centuries, peaking in the nineteenth century, but the mines are silent now. The Romans were among the first to mine here, and radiocarbon dating of slag confirms there was a Roman smelting furnace close to the fortlet at nearby Erglodd.

On the hills to the east of the village is Bedd Taliesin, a Bronze Age cairn that local legend claims is the grave of the sixth-century poet Taliesin.

After passing the **school** on the northern edge of **Tre Taliesin**, take a narrow lane on the right. This is just before the large **chapel**. Follow the lane round to the left and then turn right when you come out on a minor road. Walk downhill for about 150 metres.

10 Go through a kissing-gate, partly hidden by a tree, on the left. Walk with the fence and drainage ditch (**Pwll Ddu**) on your left across two large fields. You lose the fence beyond a kissing-gate, but Pwll Ddu remains. In fact,

Non-standard bog: *Cors Fochno, or Borth Bog, is one of the finest raised peat bogs in Britain*

the ditch is your companion for about 3.5 kilometres in total. Beyond the next gate, the belt of trees on the right disappears. The dead-straight route crosses another couple of fields before heading out on to the marsh proper.

Just before you reach a stile beside a wooden gate, there is a short section of **boardwalk** leading up to a **viewing platform** to the right of the path. It's worth the brief detour if only to get a better sense of the scale of the bog.

Cors Fochno *is one of the largest peat bogs in lowland Britain, and, as such, is protected as a National Nature Reserve. The wet, acidic soil, low in nutrients, means that only specially adapted species can survive here. These include bog rosemary, sundew, cotton grass, large heath butterfly, rosy marsh moth, bog bush cricket, otters and adders. A total of 15 sphagnum mosses grow on Cors Fochno, including three nationally rare species. Bird enthusiasts should have their binoculars handy as they cross the edge of the marsh: a number of wetland species thrive here and, in the winter, endangered hen harriers can be seen hunting on the marsh.*

11 Having passed beyond the gate/stile, you will see a bridge across **Pwll Du** on your left. Cross this. Walk with the fence on your right and then turn right through a set of gates — normally left open. A clear path cuts through an area of coarse grasses and gorse, the dampest stretches easily negotiated by sections of boardwalk. After crossing the next gated bridge, turn left along a track. On reaching a gate, go right to walk with the fence on your left. Ignoring a bridge on the left in the field corner, turn right again to continue beside the fence. Cross the next bridge on your left. Turn left, go through the gate and then climb on to the **embankment**.

12 Almost immediately, cross the **metal bridge** over the **Afon Leri** and turn right along the track. Bear left just before the large gate and maintain a straight line until you reach a **church**.

As well as the normal cemetery within the **churchyard** *itself, several pets have been buried just outside the church walls — some with simple wooden or stone grave markers, but several bearing inscribed headstones.*

From the church, turn right along the broad, sealed path. Cross the railway line and follow the path round to the road along the seafront in **Borth**.

13 You have a choice now: either turn left and follow the road to today's end point, or you can drop on to the pebbly beach and follow that south. (But the beach is very pebbly and dogs are banned from May to October.) Either way, it's just less than one kilometre to the **RNLI's Borth lifeboat station** where today's section ends.

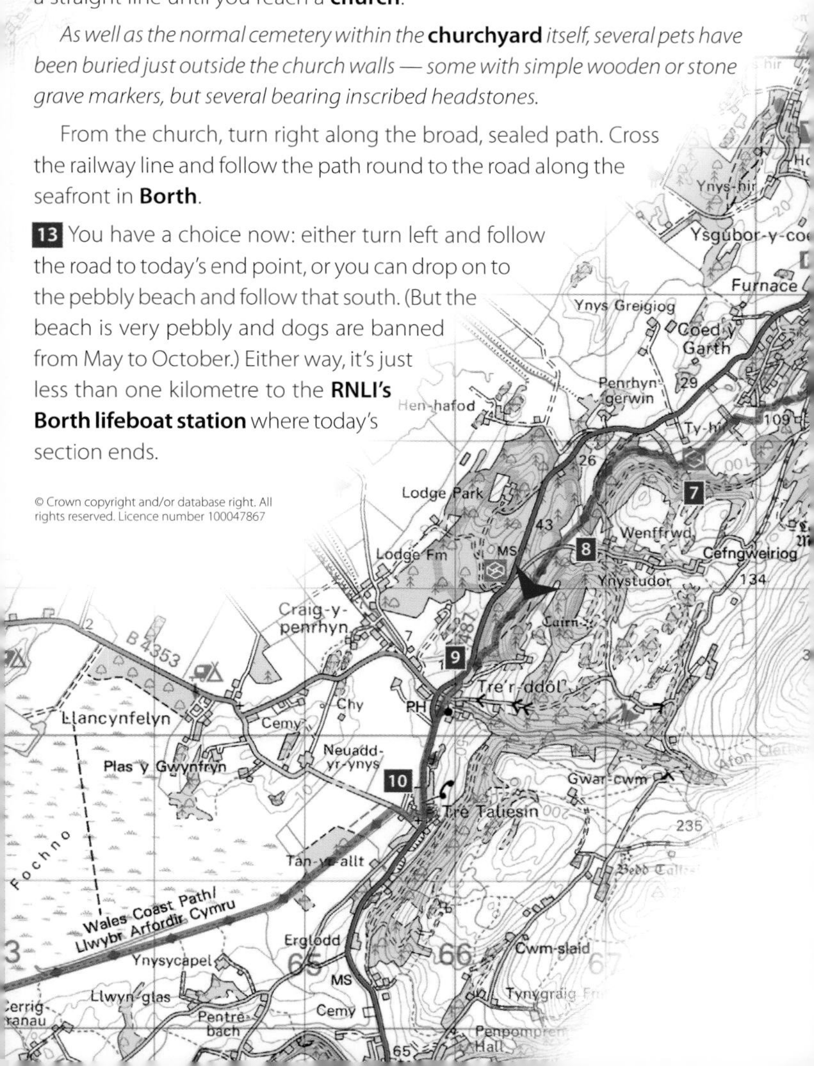

Detour: *Dyfi-Ynyslas National Nature Reserve (for details of species and habitats, see blue panel on page 131)*

Head north when you reach the coast road at **Borth 13**. To walk the **beach**, turn right, find a gap in the sea wall and drop on to the beach to follow it north. This is really only practical when the tide is out and you don't need to keep leaping over the groynes on this stretch. To bypass the groynes and join the beach further north, turn right and walk along the road for 2.5 kilometres — until you reach a fork. Bear left here and then, immediately after the bus shelter, take the track across the golf course on the left. This leads to the beach, along which you turn right. Whether you walked the beach or the road from Borth, you'll now need to watch carefully for a **wooden viewing platform** high up in the dunes — set back slightly from the beach. Nearing this point, you'll see a pole with a small red flag on it at the back of the beach. Head inland here, on a path through the dunes as far as the viewing platform. From here, pick up a clearer path — on a boardwalk at first — that leads to the **Dyfi-Ynyslas National Nature Reserve visitor centre**. (This has public toilets and a small cafe, but is open only from Easter to the end of September).

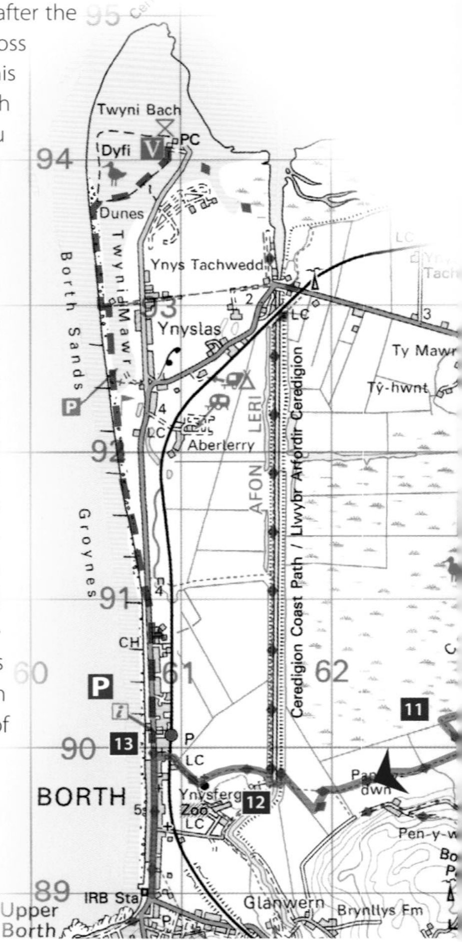

The Ceredigion Coast Path

Part of the Wales Coast Path

Dropping down the coastal path into Cwmtydu

Borth (or Ynyslas) to Aberystwyth

Distance: *10 kilometres / 6 miles (or 15 kilometres / 9 miles)* | **Start:** *RNLI lifeboat station in Borth SN 608 889 (or Dyfi-Ynyslas National Nature Reserve visitor centre SN 609 941)* | **Finish:** *Royal Pier, Aberystwyth SN 581 818* | **Maps:** *Ordnance Survey Explorer OL23 Cadair Idris & Llyn Tegid, and 213 Aberystwyth & Cwm Rheidol, Landranger 135 Aberystwyth and Machynlleth*

Outline: Beyond Borth, a rugged cliff-top route is followed to Aberystwyth, dropping to sea level only briefly at Wallog and Clarach Bay.

Those who think coastal walking is all about cliffs will love today — the first such dramatic coastal scenery since leaving Porthmadog. After leaving Borth, the route climbs quickly and then undulates all the way to Aberystwyth, passing some interesting coastal landforms along the way. The views from here are far-reaching, promising many excellent days' walking ahead

Services: *Borth has places to eat, a cash machine, shops, public toilets and accommodation, including several campsites and a youth hostel. En route to Aberystwyth, there are holiday parks, a campsite and fast food at Clarach Bay. The café on Constitution Hill is open daily from mid-January until the end of November. Aberystwyth is the largest settlement between Porthmadog and Cardigan and has a wide range of facilities including all sorts of accommodation, places to eat, cash machines, shops, public toilets and launderettes. (Aberystwyth Tourist Information Centre, Terrace Road | 01970 612125 | aberystwythtic@ceredigion.gov.uk). Aberystwyth is the last town on the route that has a railway station. Cymru Cabs, Aberystwyth | 07951 580227*

Don't miss: Borth Station Museum – railway history | **Aberystwyth Constitution Hill** – camera obscura | **Cliff railway** – funicular route

▲ *On the cliffs south of Borth*

Borth

Borth is built at the southern end of a long pebble spit, created by the processes of longshore drift, that stretches as far north as the Dyfi estuary. The village developed largely as a result of the abundance of herrings in local waters. There's no harbour though: fishermen simply built their homes right at the top of the pebble ridge and pulled their boats on to the beach. With the stormy Irish Sea on one side and the bogs of Cors Fochno on the other, it must've been a harsh, bleak existence.

An unusual period in the village's history started in 1875 when the boys and masters of the Rutland-based public school Uppingham were relocated to Borth during a typhoid epidemic. They stayed for 14 months.

Among the main attractions of Borth, other than its beach and the Dyfi-Ynyslas National Nature Reserve, are a small zoo (www.borthzoo.co.uk) and a railway museum (www.borthstationmuseum.co.uk). Although temporarily closed at the time of writing, the latter is housed in the station building, which had been derelict until 2011 when it was restored by local volunteers. It includes a renovated ticket office, restored to how it would've looked in the 1950s, and displays relating to railway history.

Borth seen from the cliffs

The route: **Borth (or Ynyslas) to Aberystwyth**

From Ynyslas (Ceredigion Coast Path):
The official **Ceredigion Coast Path**, which predates the Wales Coast Path, coincides with the Wales Coast Path for much of its distance. The only difference is that the northernmost point of the former is **Ynyslas**, whereas the latter rejoins the coast at Borth and then heads south, missing out Ynyslas. Those who wish to walk the Ceredigion Coast Path in its entirety need to start today's section from the **Dyfi-Ynyslas National Nature Reserve visitor centre** at Ynyslas.

Standing on the south side of the visitor centre, with your back to the building, take the path through the small gate on the right. This leads out through the dunes and past a wooden viewing platform to drop down a shingle slope to the beach. Turn left along the beach.

Walkers now have two options. If tide times permit, the beach can be followed south (**route A on the map**) for almost 4.5 kilometres — as far as the **RNLI lifeboat station** in Borth. (When you first reach Borth, you may wish to use the road rather than the beach, which is very pebbly and has a dog ban on it from May to October.)

Alternatively (**route B on the map**), walk south along the beach for 700 metres and then, when you see a **small building** just above the beach, join the Ceredigion Coast Path inland option. This involves leaving the beach here and picking up a **track** to the right of the building. This crosses the **golf course** and then goes straight over a **minor road**. Following a dead-straight line, continue ahead on a rough track that becomes a grassy path, passing through a number of gates.

On reaching a **surfaced lane**, keep straight ahead. Turn left along the **B4353** and then, immediately after the **level crossing**, take the walkway on the right, running beside the **railway**.

Sunken land: *Towards Ynyslas, an ancient submerged forest is sometimes revealed at low tide*

Immediately after crossing the **Afon Leri**, go through the kissing-gate on the left. After walking along the top of the raised embankment beside the river for about 3 kilometres, go through a large gate and turn right. Maintain a straight line until you reach a church. Now turn right along the broad, sealed path. Cross the railway line and follow the path round to the **B4353** in **Borth**.

Either follow the road or the beach left as far as the **RNLI lifeboat station** in **Borth**.

Ynyslas

This National Nature Reserve covers a massive 2,000 hectares, taking in estuarine habitats, sand dunes and the raised bog of Cors Fochno. It is home to four of the UK's six native reptiles: common lizards, sand lizards, adders and grass snakes. In summer, watch for a variety of butterflies, day-flying moths and, over the bog, dragonflies. You may even spot osprey and otter on the estuary.

From Borth (Wales Coast Path):

1 From the RNLI lifeboat station in Borth, head south — either by dropping back on to the beach or continuing along the seafront road. Whichever you choose, you then need to walk up **Cliff Road**. This is the next turning on the right if you are walking on the road; if you are on the beach, you need to come up at the next opportunity beyond the lifeboat station and then turn sharp right. When the road ends, keep to the seaward side of the unusual, white house.

2 Cliffs! At last, we have reached the first of the cliffs along the Cardigan Bay section of the Wales Coast Path. And, generally speaking, it's now cliff-top walking, with the sea breeze in your hair, all the way to Cardigan. Being careful not to stray too close to the crumbly cliff edge, follow the path uphill to the **war memorial** above Borth. There is also a coin-operated telescope here if the weather's clear — and you have a spare twenty pence piece. Training the telescope on the north, you're able to look across the Afon Dyfi to the southernmost mountains of Snowdonia, including the Tarren hills, running down to the sea at Aberdyfi.

From the memorial, the path drops to cross a stream at the back of a **tiny cove**. A clear, zig-zagging path

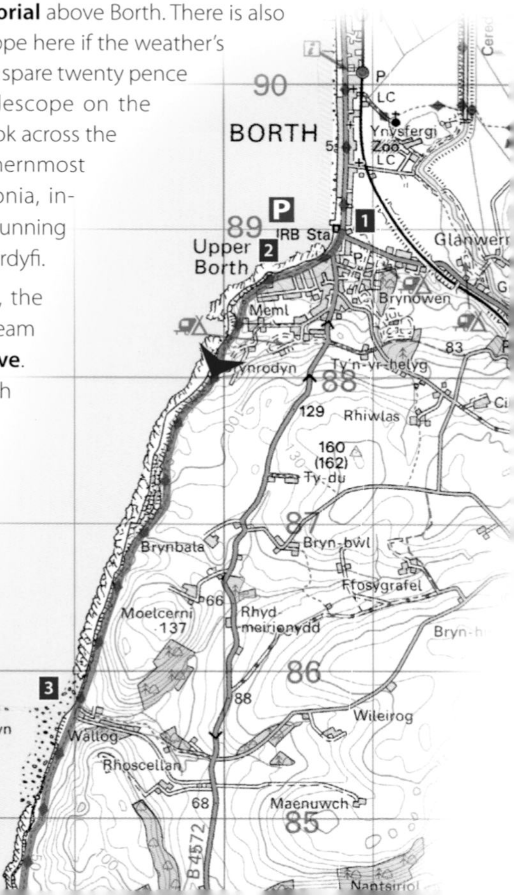

Over the sea: *On the cliff path heading south*

climbs out the other side. Don't be tempted to cut any corners — some lead to trouble. Don't even be put off by the stile ahead with a private sign on it; go right up to it, and then, instead of crossing it, climb the steps on the right, seemingly invisible until the very last moment.

Geology enthusiasts will find the next stretch of coast fascinating. The cliffs consist largely of Borth mudstones and Aberystwyth grits, sedimentary rocks deposited in the early Silurian period as a result of particularly turbulent, sediment-laden submarine currents triggered by an earthquake or storm.

The two come up against each other at Craig y Delyn, or Harp Rock, where the Aberystwyth grits form a great sloping slab with the strata resembling harp strings.

Beyond the steps, the cliff path climbs at a gentler angle. It's a long, slow climb with just a couple of dips in it. Watch for **Craig y Delyn** along the way.

3 The next significant landmark on the coast path is the **large, detached house at Wallog**, occupying a truly enviable spot at the back of the beach. After crossing some low cliffs just before the house, go through a gate just back from the cliff edge. Cross the **bridge** over the stream, turn right and immediately go left along a narrow path beside the retaining wall of the house.

Stretching out into the water from Wallog is Sarn Gynfelyn, a spit of what is thought to be glacial moraine. At low tide, the spit resembles a manmade cause-

way, but it is entirely natural. When the water is calm, you can just about make out the mild undulations on the water's surface, marking the line of it stretching into the distance. It is thought to run for about 11 kilometres, ending at an underwater reef known as the Patches. Sarn Gynfelyn is associated with the Atlantis-style legend of the lost kingdom of Cantre'r Gwaelod, said to lie beneath Cardigan Bay.

As it begins climbing again, the path passes just above a well-preserved **lime kiln**.

There are many lime kilns along the southwest coast of Wales. Most of them are fairly small, set up by individual farmers to fertilise the land. In Ceredigion, small sailing ships would've brought limestone from Pembrokeshire and unloaded it in small bays and inlets. It would then have been burned with coal and clay to produce lime for the fields. This counteracted excessive acidity in the soil and enabled crops to be grown on marginal land.

Bottlenose dolphins are found throughout the world

Bottlenose dolphins

Intelligent creatures that gather in social 'pods'

Cardigan Bay is home to one of the two largest populations of bottlenose dolphins in British waters. The other is in the Moray Firth in northeast Scotland. Each is thought to support as many as 130 animals, although they tend to gather in smaller social units, or pods, of about 25. While individuals range further afield at certain times — indeed, they are able to cross from Wales to the Irish coast in a matter of hours — dolphins can be seen in Cardigan Bay throughout the year.

These highly intelligent creatures live for anything between 20 and 50 years. The most common of dolphin species, they are spread throughout the world. They're usually two to three metres long, although those found in British waters are often up to four metres in length.

Bottlenose dolphins live on a diet made up almost entirely of fish and squid. Working as a team or individually, they use echolocation to track down their prey. This involves emitting clicking sounds and then using the resulting echoes to locate objects. Other noises made by bottlenose dolphins include whistles and high-pitch squeaks.

More information: The Sea Watch Foundation has more on the bottlenose dolphin's distribution and lifestyle at **www.seawatchfoundation.org.uk**

Bird's eye view: *Aberystwyth from Constitution Hill*

The practice dates back to the Middle Ages and continued well into the nineteenth century — until artificial fertilisers began to replace traditional methods. The lime produced would probably also have been used to make mortar for building and whitewash for painting walls.

4 About 1.5 kilometres beyond Wallog, the route drops to **Clarach Bay** — not a place to linger unless you're thinking of visiting the beach and having a look at the complex folding in the low cliffs to the north.

Pass between the holiday village buildings on the northern edge of the bay and then cross the **footbridge** over **Afon Clarach**. Walk beside an access lane, past the amusements and a burger bar. Keep to this lane for now — as it swings away from the beach and begins to head uphill.

5 As the lane bends left, take the well-signposted path to **Aberystwyth** on the right. This constructed path, with several benches beside it, leads all the way to **Constitution Hill** overlooking the town.

The hill, with its excellent views north to the Llŷn peninsula and out across the town to the south, is crowned by a camera obscura as well as a café.

An electric **funicular cliff railway**, the longest of its type in Britain, brings

visitors up from the esplanade below. You'll see the **café** and other buildings just to the left of the path. Continue downhill on bare rock, soon joining a stepped path that follows a zig-zagging route down the slope, criss-crossing over the funicular railway. At the bottom of the path, turn right to drop to the **seafront**. Go left and follow the broad walkway all the way to Aberystwyth's small **Royal Pier** where today's section ends.

Constitution Hill

Aberystwyth Cliff Railway has been taking visitors up and down Constitution Hill since 1896. The camera obscura on the summit is more recent — it dates from 1985 and has a 35-centimetre lens, making it one of the largest in the world. Aberystwyth's first camera obscura *was built in 1880 in the grounds of the castle but was later moved to Constitution Hill to take advantage of the superb views.*

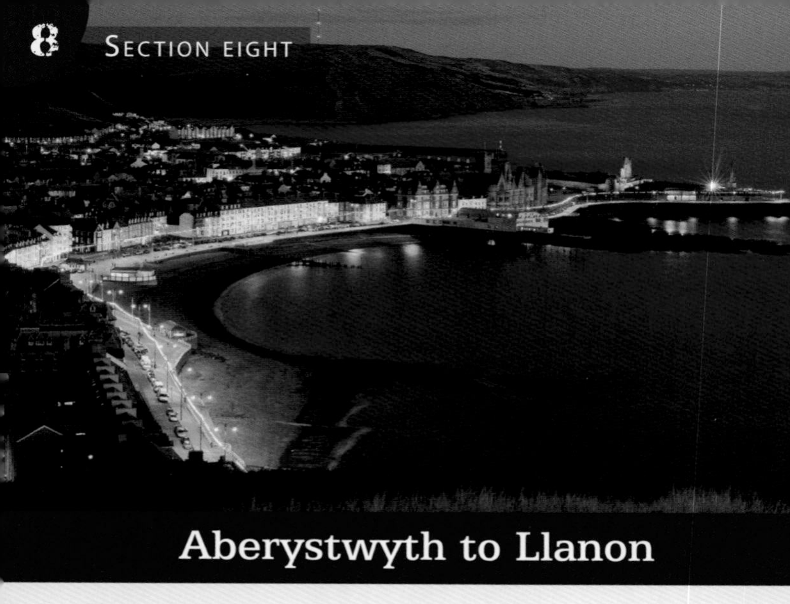

Aberystwyth to Llanon

Distance: *21 kilometres / 13 miles* | **Start:** *Royal Pier, Aberystwyth SN 581 818* **Finish:** *Beach car park by Afon Cledan, Llanon SN 507 667* | **Maps:** *Ordnance Survey Explorers 213 Aberystwyth & Cwm Rheidol and 199 Lampeter, Landranger 135 Aberystwyth and Machynlleth*

Outline: An atmospheric day of cliff-top walking interspersed with gently rolling farmland and bracken-clad slopes just back from the precipice.

Soon after leaving Aberystwyth, the route heads back onto cliffs and heathland. The lack of villages, ruined farmhouses and a wealth of wildlife give this section an isolated feel. It sometimes follows ancient ways where the incessant passage of travellers has worn a groove into the grassy hillsides. A brief return to civilisation — and the main road — at Llanrhystud is followed by a return to the sea, and a walk through farmland to reach Llanon.

Services: *Aberystwyth is the largest place between Porthmadog and Cardigan and has lots of facilities including accommodation, places to eat, cash machines, shops, public toilets and launderettes. (Aberystwyth Tourist Information Centre, Terrace Road | 01970 612125 | aberystwythtic@ceredigion.gov.uk). There are few facilities en route today, apart from at Llanrhystud, where there are shops, accommodation (including a campsite) and a pub that serves food. Llanon, at day's end, has some facilities including accommodation, a pub, a shop and takeaway food, but the choice is limited. Aberystwyth is the last town with a railway station, but there are regular buses between Aberystwyth and Llanrhystud/Llanon. Cymru Cabs, Aberystwyth | 07951 580227*

Don't miss: **Aberystwyth Castle** – thirteenth-century ruins | **Pen Dinas** – prehistoric remains | **Penderi Nature Reserve** – cliff-face oak woodland

▲ *Aberystwyth at night*

Aberystwyth

There have been people living in and around modern-day Aberystwyth for many millennia: evidence of Iron Age, Bronze Age and even Mesolithic people has been found in the area. Much later, a settlement grew up around the castle. During the seventeenth century, this housed a Royal Mint, attracting the wrath of Cromwell's forces in 1649. Most of the buildings seen today in Aberystwyth were constructed during the nineteenth century.

Education has been an important part of life in the town since 1867 when a committee formed to establish a university in Wales bought the troubled Castle Hotel for £10,000. Within five years, it'd been converted to a college and opened as University College Wales — with just 26 students and three teaching staff. Since then, the university has changed its name on several occasions and moved to a considerably larger campus. Today, as Aberystwyth University, it has about 8,000 students — who make up about one-third of the town's population

As well as the university, Aberystwyth is home to the National Library of Wales. Purpose built in 1915, it now holds more than 6.5 million books and periodicals, as well as the national collection of Welsh manuscripts.

Aberystwyth seafront including castle ruins and the Old College

Scholarly: *The university town of Aberystwyth seen from the south*

The route: **Aberystwyth to Llanon**

1 With your back to the entrance to the **Royal Pier** in **Aberystwyth**, turn right along the seafront **promenade**. The rather grand, mock-Gothic building on your left in a short while is the **Old College**, standing on the site of Castle House. This was built in 1865 as a hotel but was converted into a college in 1872 after financial difficulties. Straight ahead are the remains of the town's thirteenth-century castle. As you continue along the seafront, keep to the right of the castle and the imposing **war memorial**, designed in the 1920s by Italian sculptor Mario Rutelli. There are plenty of benches along this stretch of the promenade, as well as pay-to-view telescopes: plenty of opportunity to enjoy the coastal scenery.

2 Keep to the seafront until you see the **marina** to your left. Just before entering the pay-and-display parking area, turn left along **Quay Road**. Ignoring any turnings to the left, you swing around the side of a **small harbour** inlet and pass to the left of a car/boat park. The passageway narrows as it passes to the left of the orange-brick Welsh Water pumping station. Immediately turn left up a narrow set of steps beside a white building, which turns out to be a wine bar. Go right at the top of the steps and then, emerging on the main road, turn right again to cross the **Afon Rheidol**.

3 Immediately after the **bridge**, head off to the right. Ignoring the steps, head almost back on yourself along a surfaced walkway. Keep to the left of the **Aberystwyth Justice Centre**. Continue on another walkway between waterside homes on your left and the **marina** on your right. Go through a gap in a low wooden fence to keep close to the water. Keeping right when the lane forks, you soon join a quiet road, along which you bear right.

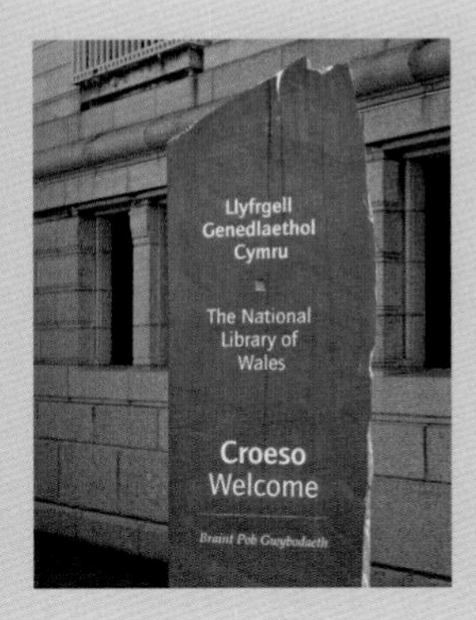

Wartime haven

During World War Two, many of Britain's treasures were evacuated to Aberystwyth for safe-keeping by the National Library of Wales. The British Museum, the National Gallery and Cambridge's Corpus Christi College were among the institutes that took advantage of the underground depository, sending items that included the Magna Carta, original Shakespeare manuscripts and drawings by Leonardo da Vinci.

4 As you cross the **bridge** over the **Afon Ystwyth**, you finally have a sense of leaving the confines of Aberystwyth behind. Head left across the parking area and then continue beyond the barrier on a broad, stony track.

Up to the left is the pepper pot-like Wellington Monument, built by public subscription in the 1850s as a memorial to the Duke of Wellington, the victor of Waterloo who died in 1852. The hill on which it stands, Pen Dinas, is also home to an Iron Age fort and a Bronze Age burial mound. Evidence of even earlier peoples has been found on Tanybwlch Beach close to the base of the hill: the flint tools and weapons of Mesolithic people who were here between 7,000 and 9,000 years ago.

The substantial shingle spit on your right is not a particularly attractive feature, but is important for wildlife nonetheless. It is, in fact, a Site of Special Scientific Interest, protected largely because of the unusual plants that grow here, including a fairly unusual prostrate blackthorn and sea radish, a yellow-flowered member of the brassica family that can grow to about 1.5 metres in height. Watch for waders on the beach, including oystercatchers, turnstones, sanderlings and ringed plovers, which lay their eggs on the shingle. There are also choughs in this area.

The first climb of the day looms ahead: **Allt-wen**. As you ascend, keep to the right of the fence — on a well-walked path up the grassy hillside. The first part of the climb is very steep, but is rewarded near the top with a glimpse of the exposed rock face — revealed by nineteenth-century quarrying.

Mellow yellow: *Looking down over Afon Ystwyth to the coast path south of Aberystwyth*

Stone was once carried from these quarries via a horse-drawn tramway behind Tanybwlch Beach.

Before too long, you're striding out along the gently undulating cliff-top with views inland of villages nestling in wooded valleys and backed by hills rolling away into the distance.

After a kissing-gate, you begin a long, gentle descent towards the **Morfa Bychan Holiday Park** on a broad carpet of soft grass. *Morfa Bychan was once a grange of the Strata Florida Abbey, several kilometres inland. Rhys Ddu, one of Welsh leader Owain Glyndŵr's most loyal commanders, once lived here. He was captured by the English and executed in London.*

Reaching the edge of the caravan site, go through a green kissing-gate, over a small bridge and then head up the slope to the left. A series of way-markers indicates the route through stands of bracken and gorse. Hawthorn bushes bent double by the prevailing south-westerlies are testament to the strength and persistence of the winds along this section of the Welsh coast.

5 After a kissing-gate next to a larger metal gate, turn left along the holiday park's access lane. Almost immediately, step off to the right and head up through a kissing-gate. Walk straight up the hillside on a broad, grassy swathe through the bracken and gorse. It cuts across an old **stone embankment**.

Go straight over at a crossing of paths, resisting the urge to head seaward again. The path winds its way up to a surfaced lane. Turn right along this and then right again — along a rough track to **Llety'r Gegin Farm**.

6 About 350 metres beyond the farm, the track swings sharp right. As it does so, go through the waymarked bridle-gate on the left. A broad, grassy path heads downhill between two fences. After going through a gate, you lose the fences but the route is now delightfully delineated by hawthorn bushes forming a guard of honour over your head. *In the autumn, birds flit from bush to bush, picking at the succulent haws.*

7 Nearing the abandoned farm at **Ffos-lâs**, the path heads quickly up the slope on the left and then continues parallel with a fence down to the right. It passes to the left of the buildings and then bears left along another excellent, grassy track. About 180 metres beyond the ruins, bear right along a narrower path. In another 80 metres, any semblance of a clear path disappears as you drop down to the right — along the top of an **embankment** — to reach a kissing-gate. Once through this, head straight towards the sea and then turn left along the top of the low, crumbly cliffs. Finally, another inland detour is over. As pleasant as it was at times, it's great to be back out on the cliffs again!

Keep close to the fence on your right until you reach a small ravine just below the buildings of **Mynachdy'r-graig**. *Like Morfa Bychan, Mynachdy'r-graig was once owned by the monks of Strata Florida. Its name translates as 'monk's house on the rocks'. Today, the house itself is in private hands, but the land to the southwest is owned by the National Trust.*

Looking back towards Aberystwyth and the Wellington Monument on Pen Dinas

Guard of honour: *Blackthorn and gorse flanking the coast path*

8 Turn sharp left to head uphill, through a kissing-gate, over a **plank bridge** and up to a fingerpost. Turn right here, soon passing in front of the farmhouse. Follow a rough track uphill, but only for about 50 metres; you need to strike off right, along a path beside a fence. You lose the fence after a wooden kissing-gate, but the onward path is obvious as it steadily ascends the bracken and gorse-covered hillside. Having gained some height, the views of the distant cliffs are mesmerising.

The path passes above a wooden step stile leading on to the nature reserve at the **Penderi Cliffs**.

A path on the other side of the fence allows a glimpse of hanging oak woodland, an area of sessile oaks whose growth has been severely stunted by the salt-laden winds. Other native woodland species here include small-leaved lime, rowan, hazel, wych elm and spindle. It's an interesting sight, particularly in spring and early summer when the wildflowers, such as wood anemone, bluebell, red campion and greater stitchwort are in flower. There aren't many areas of hanging oak left, but the Wildlife Trust is trying to protect the few remaining fragments. You can visit the woodland, but you'll need to backtrack to this stile because the path doesn't continue.

About 100 metres after passing above the stile into the reserve, the broad,

Roller-coaster: *Undulating cliffs between Aberystwyth and Llanrhystud*

grassy path swings away to the left. Leave it here by continuing straight on — along a narrower trail that soon passes to the right of large pile of stones. Go through a gate to head along the top of the high, impressive **Penderi Cliffs**, also part of the nature reserve. *In summer, watch and listen for nesting seabirds, including cormorants, shags and fulmars.*

Beyond the next kissing-gate, the path cuts across the grassy hillside. Having gone through several more gates, it drops steeply to cross a **wooden footbridge** over a tiny stream, practically dry in the height of summer. A white-topped post on the slope opposite indicates your onward route. Without a guiding path on the ground, head up the grassy slope to a fence, and then walk with this on your left, later dropping down a steep slope to pass through a kissing-gate.

Walk with the fence on your right, carefully avoiding the rabbit holes. When the fence starts dropping away, veer half left and go through yet another kissing-gate. Now on the seaward side of the fence, the coast path follows an undulating route along the dramatic cliff-top. At low tide, look back for a glimpse of hidden shingle coves.

The sight of another large caravan park ahead heralds the start of a long, gentle descent from the high cliffs. After a **bridge**, the trail heads to the right.

Just beyond a particularly badly eroded section of cliff, it swings up to the left, through a kissing-gate and onward to a fingerpost in the gorse. Turn right at the fingerpost. Having gone through a couple of kissing-gates, the path passes above the **Pengarreg Caravan Park**. A faint trail keeps close to the brambles on your left and then swings right to drop on to an access track at the far end of the line of caravans. Turn left along this and then head left along the main access lane, passing the **shop and reception**. Follow the surfaced lane all the way to the road.

9 Those ending this leg of the coast path in **Llanrhystud** should turn left on reaching the **A487**. Otherwise, to continue on the main route, turn right along the single-track lane towards **Morfa Farm caravan park**. Follow the lane until it ends at a parking area.

10 The coast path now heads left along the top of a shingle ridge at the back of a long beach. After about 400 metres, drop left off the shingle and then walk along the field edge. At the far end of the second field, go through the gate and then follow the trail left — away from the beach. Ignoring a path to the left, pass to the right of a **group of limekilns** at **Craig-las**. *These kilns are quite different to the single kilns often encountered at small inlets along the coast. The latter would've been for the use of a single farm, but these four kilns operated on a larger scale. They were served by boats unloading limestone and coal via the jetty below — an industry that continued until the early part of the twentieth century.*

The tranquil coast north of Llanrhystud

After a gate, you're back out in the open again, with the waves lapping up against the beach directly below. After the next kissing-gate, bear left. Keep close to the boundary on your left as you cross two fields, often full of cattle. Beyond the second field, a muddy track leads straight towards the church in **Llansantffraed**.

For those who like mooching around churchyards, Llansantffraed's is home to some interesting gravestones, including those of several dozen local mariners who died at sea and a Spanish ship's captain whose body washed ashore nearby in 1916.

11 On reaching the **church**, follow the lane over the **bridge**. There is a choice of routes now. To avoid a potentially difficult stream crossing on the beach, see the 'inland alternative' described below. The main coast path, however, goes sharp right. It then heads left along **Heol-yr-Esgob**. Keep straight ahead as the surfaced lane goes over to rough track, and then continue beyond the bungalows, with a fence on your left. Descend the **metal steps** and then

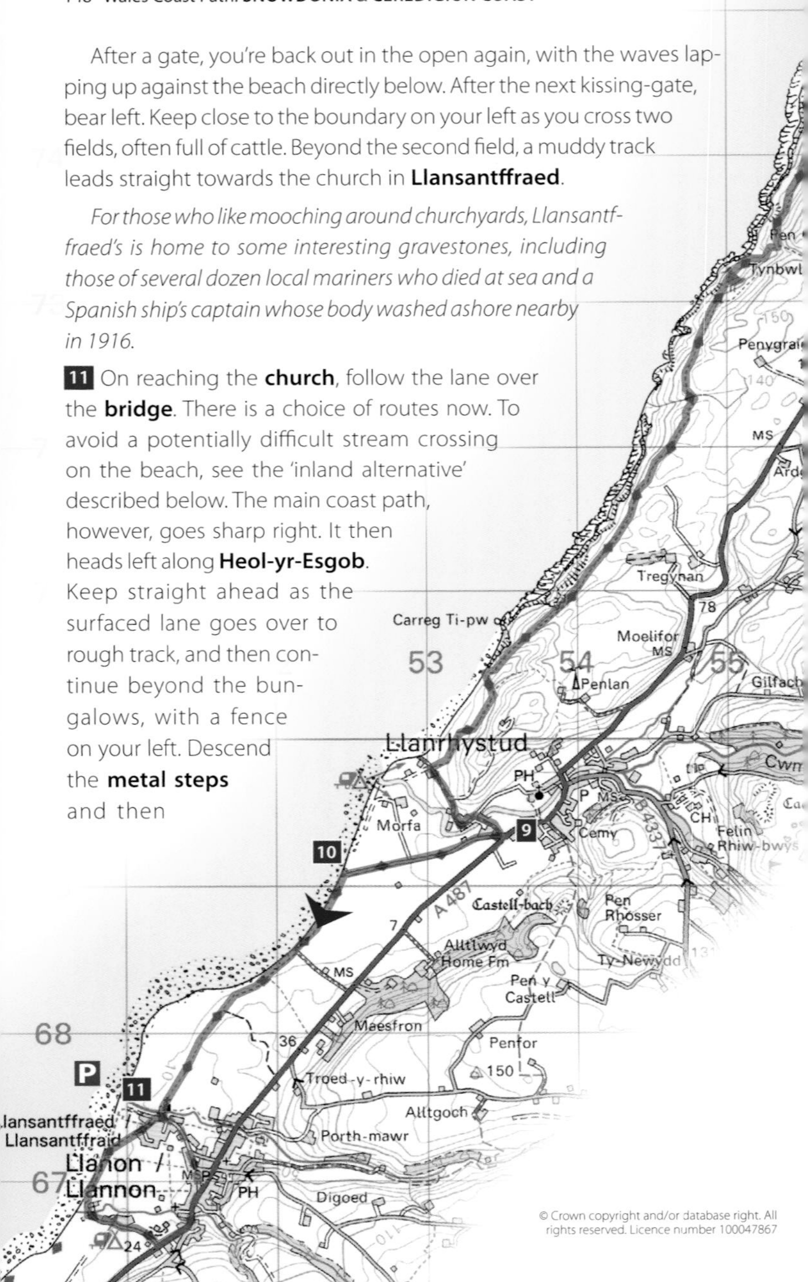

Quiet coast: *Looking back over Llansantfraed from the hills to the south*

turn left along the shingle beach. Continue past the next set of steps, only leaving the beach after crossing the **Afon Cledan** as it enters the sea. (The steps could be used as an escape route inland to Llanon if the river crossing is too tricky — as it can sometimes be after heavy rain.) Today's section ends in the **small car park** on the south side of the Afon Cledan.

From the car park, those spending the night in Llanon will need to follow the lane up to the main road and then turn left. It's about 600 metres from the car park to the centre of the village.

Alternative inland route: *avoiding difficult stream crossing on beach*

After crossing the bridge just below the church in Llansantffraed, bear left along the lane and then go right at the main road. Head through Llanon and then take the road on the right about 250 metres after passing the 40mph sign. This drops to the parking area where today's section ends. The inland alternative adds about 600 metres to today's total distance.

Llanon to New Quay

Distance: *18 kilometres / 11 miles* | **Start:** *Beach car park beside Afon Cledan, Llanon SN 507 667* | **Finish:** *The Corner Shop and Post Office, South John Street, New Quay SH 389 600* | **Maps:** *Ordnance Survey Explorers 199 Lampeter and 198 Cardigan and New Quay, Landrangers 135 Aberystwyth and Machynlleth, 146 Lampeter and Llandovery and 145 Cardigan and Mynydd Preseli*

Outline: A roller-coaster walk along cliffs, across farmland and in and out of wooded ravines — with Aberaeron providing a half-way break.

After the sense of isolation experienced yesterday, section nine feels a lot less remote. For the first seven kilometres or so, you're never far from the main road and much of the route keeps close to farmland. Things change beyond Aberaeron. Now the route follows excellent cliff-top paths, dipping in and out of attractive ravines and passing through the cool shade of woods as it nears New Quay. At low tide, much of the final few kilometres are on a beach.

Services: *Llanon's facilities include accommodation, a pub, a shop and takeaway food. Aberaeron has a wider selection of places to stay as well as pubs, cafés and shops. It also has a campsite, public toilets and cash machine. New Quay is also geared up for tourists with a decent range of places to stay and eat, shops, public toilets and cash machine. Cymru Cabs, Aberystwyth | 07951 580227*

Don't miss: **Fish traps** – medieval remains | **Aberaeron** – attractive harbour | **New Quay Bay** – long, sandy beaches

▲ *Aberaeron at night*

Llanon

At first glance, Llanon seems an unimpressive place, but you don't have to dig deep to discover its history and its mysteries. The place name is closely associated with St Non, the mother of St David. (Alternatively, it could translate as 'church of the ash tree'.) Some even believe St David was brought up here, although another Llanon in Carmarthenshire makes the same claim. The ruins of a Tudor building in the village, known as Y Neuadd, are thought to occupy the site of the original St Non's chapel.

Nearby is a traditional, eighteenth-century cottage with its original straw rope under-thatch still in place, one of the last surviving buildings of its type in west Wales. Managed by Ceredigion Museum, the simple, two-room cottage is open to the public during some school holidays.

One of the most fascinating of Llanon's features is its medieval strip field system. North of the Afon Cledan are 140 narrow ribbons of land, known as furlongs or slangs, that were once farmed by serfs on behalf of the bishops of St Davids. Instead of being taken over by a single landowner when the bishops relinquished control, many different local families continued farming them, ensuring they were never consolidated.

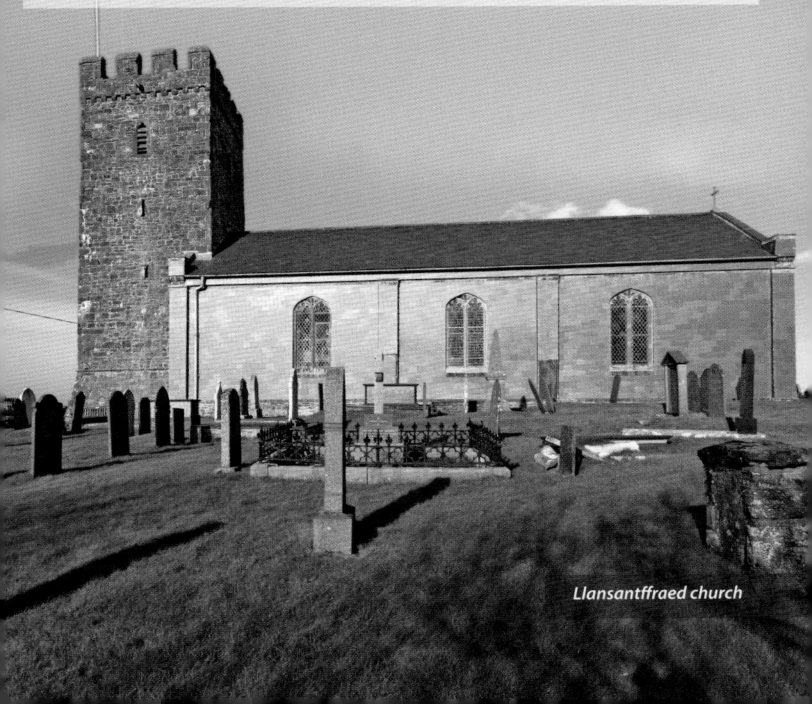

Llansantffraed church

The route: Llanon to New Quay

1 Go through the pedestrian gate at the back of the **beach car park** beside the **Afon Cledan** and follow the path southwest along the seaward edge of several fields. Beyond this flat area of arable land, the path heads a few metres inland to go through a kissing-gate and ford a small stream. Having crossed, make your way back towards the sea. As indicated by a fingerpost, the path now begins gently ascending open pasture, heading towards the **cliffs of Graig Ddu**. Keep back from the crumbly cliff edge here.

When the tide is out, **medieval fish traps** *can sometimes be glimpsed in the shallow waters along this stretch of coast. These pools were built by the Cistercian monks of Strata Florida Abbey. With low walls on three sides, topped by wattle fences, they became submerged at high tide, trapping the fish when the water later receded.*

The gently sloping grassland gives way to steeper, bracken-covered slopes beyond two gates in quick succession, but the going remains relatively easy for now. This gorgeous balcony path, occupying a broad ledge on the hillside with the waves crashing below, makes for superb walking — despite one or two muddy patches. When it ends, keep close to the fence on your right until a waymarker post tells you to head inland. About 50 metres beyond the post, drop sharp right towards the village of **Aberarth**.

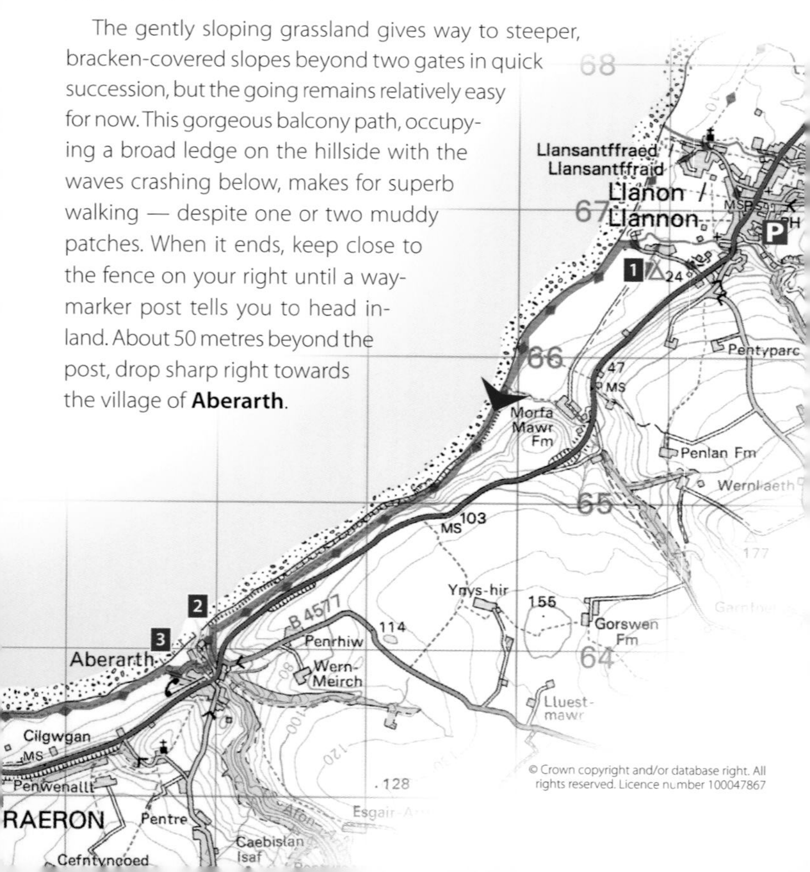

Bear river: *Aberarth is a small village just north of Aberaeron*

During the twelfth century, the stones to build Strata Florida Abbey were landed at Aberarth. They'd come all the way from Bath, shipped via Bristol, and then had to be carted inland for about 30 kilometres to the building site close to the source of the Afon Teifi.

2 Go through a kissing-gate and bear left to go through a second gate. Follow the rough lane to a road junction. Turn left and then, almost immediately, right along a walled path. This quickly crosses the **footbridge** over **Afon Arth**, or Bear River. Keep straight on, passing a **chapel** on your right.

Like many of the buildings in the village, the chapel was badly damaged when the Afon Arth flooded in 1846. It was rebuilt in 1848.

Follow the road round to the right, heading uphill. On reaching a T-junction, turn right. As you reach the last of the houses in the village, this little lane narrows to become a footpath. A set of steps leads down on to a long, shingly beach, but the coast path goes left to keep to the top of the low cliffs.

3 With agricultural land over the fence on the left, the coast path keeps to the cliff-top at first. It then drops on to stony ground at the back of the beach. The path eventually becomes a broad track with **sea defences** on the right as you pass a **campsite** on the edge of **Aberaeron**. Keep straight on, along the **sea wall**, as you reach a pay-and-display **parking area**.

Colourful: *The Georgian harbour town of Aberaeron*

4 Go left when you reach the **harbour's north pier**. (There are **public toilets** here and on the other side of the harbour.) Keep the harbour close by on your right as you head towards the heart of this colourful, lively little town.

Either side of the mouth of the Afon Aeron are brightly painted Georgian buildings, the homes of the captains of ships that sailed in and out of this once thriving port. The settlement started life as a small fishing port, but then, in 1807, Parliament granted Alban Thomas Jones Gwynne, Lord of the Manor of Aberaeron, permission to build a town here. Designed by the Shrewsbury-based architect Edward Haycock, it became a bustling community with shipyards, a woollen mill and small ironworks. Although its industries went into decline in the early part of the twentieth century, it has since reinvented itself as a destination for tourists.

The coast path doesn't go into the main part of the town; instead, it crosses a **footbridge** over the river close to **The Cellar restaurant and bar**. Once on the other side of the water, turn right to keep close to the **harbour**. Nearing the harbour mouth again, follow the road round to the left. Pick up a path along the top of a **shingle bank**. Then, as you pass the last of a set of houses, head up the slope on the left and immediately bear right at a fork.

The path soon climbs back on to the cliffs. It drops slightly to cross a small **ravine**. Keep right at a faint fork as the path climbs out of the dip. Later, the narrow, beaten-earth trail joins a broader, grassy path coming in from the left.

5 The next ravine you come to is the lovely, wooded valley of **Cwm Clifforch**. Beyond here, the path climbs to a metal gate. Once through this, you're on another confined path along the cliff-top. Later, coming back out into the

Palace architect

Llanerchaeron, an eighteenth-century villa just outside Aberaeron, was designed by John Nash, the Georgian architect best known for designing Buckingham Palace. Before it was left to the National Trust in 1989, the site had been home to ten generations of the Lewes family. Today, the house, walled gardens, stables, farmyard and lake form part of a popular tourist attraction.

Above the sea: *Walkers on the grassy coast path south of Aberaeron*

open again, the trail swings left, gradually coming away from the sea. Go through a kissing-gate up in the field corner to reach a surfaced lane, along which you turn right.

6 The road crosses the **Pont y Gilfach** over the **Afon Cwinten** and then swings up to the right, past a couple of cottages at **Gilfach-yr-Halen**. Take the next turning on the right — into the **holiday village**. Keep to the left of the white-washed building and you'll soon be back on a clear, broad track between hedgerows.

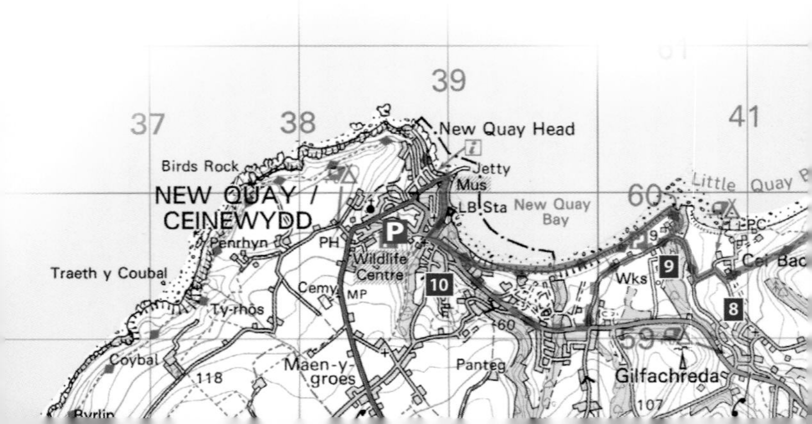

Follow this track for about 400 metres — until you encounter a gate across it. Now go through the kissing-gate on your right. Head diagonally down the slope to pass through a gap in the hedgerow. Keep to the bottom of this enclosure and then drop through a kissing-gate on the right.

7 The next ravine encountered on the coast path, containing the **Afon Drywi**, is the most interesting and attractive of the day. At the bottom of the steep descent, turn right and then fork left to cross the stream via a railed, wooden **footbridge**.

This is a charming spot: the water comes tumbling down the gorge, the steep sides of which reveal layers of sedimentary rocks uplifted over time. It then plummets over the lip of the cliff, dropping into the sea about 30 metres below.

Initially, the path climbs steeply from the Afon Drywi, but, after a kissing-gate, the incline becomes gentler. You're now on another one of those marvellous Ceredigion paths: a broad, grassy route cutting across the hillside in spectacular fashion. Sometimes, overhanging

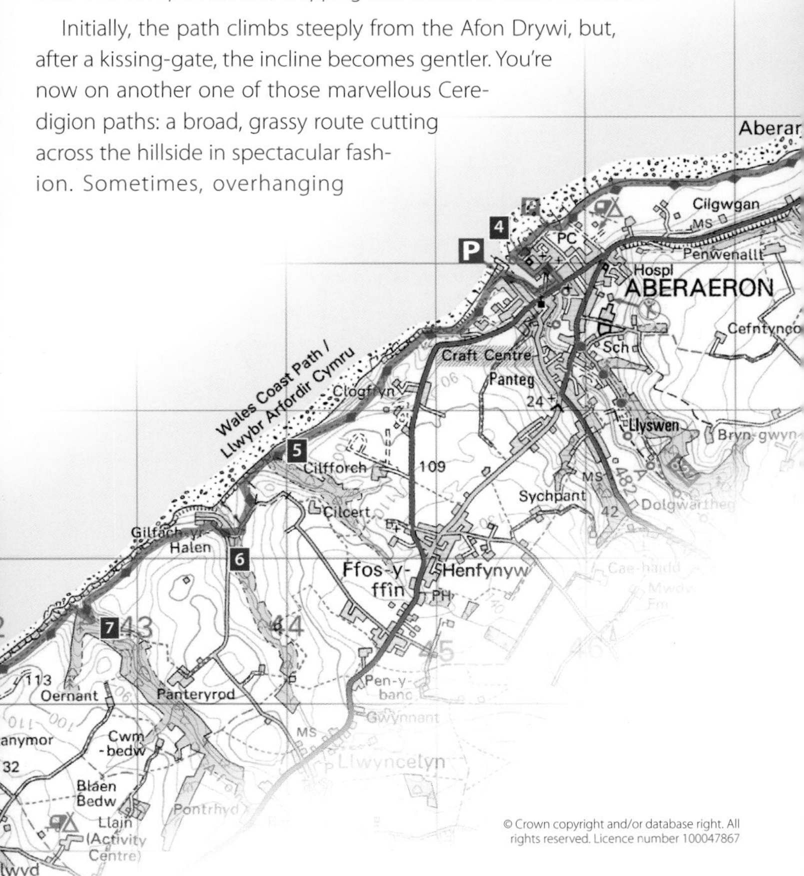

Sea views: *High above the sea on the coast path approaching New Quay*

trees and bushes provide welcome shade. As the path starts descending, there's a glorious scene ahead: the golden beaches of New Quay appear, the first significant stretches of sand we've seen in a long while, and the colourful homes of the town itself are stacked up, layer upon layer, hugging the steep slopes leading down to its sparkling bay. As you near the town, the surrounding vegetation becomes increasingly luxuriant and, occasionally, there are patches of woodland clinging to the slopes.

At a crossing of tracks, go diagonally left to continue in roughly the same direction on a constructed path. A kissing-gate leads out of the woods. As you walk with the hedgerow on your right, you'll see that you've come inland a little way. Nearing the top corner of a **static caravan park**, don't be tempted by the beaten-earth path swinging away to the left; instead, continue beside the field boundary and then go through a gate on to an enclosed path.

8 Entering a rough yard, head left, past the **farmhouse** and then go right — along a rough lane. Turn right at the T-junction with a single-track road. Ignoring a turning to the right that leads to the beach at **Cei Bach**, follow the road down to the left and then round to the right. This wooded lane drops to cross **Pont Llanina**, where the coast path splits.

9 When the tide is out, you can stroll along the beach almost all the way to **New Quay**. (For the **high-tide alternative**, see below.) To reach the beach, turn right immediately after the bridge — along the lane leading to the tiny **St Ina's Church**.

Go through the gate on the right to access a path through the trees. This soon leads down to the **beach**. Climb the steps on the breakwater and then turn left along the delightfully firm sand.

St Ina

There's debate as to whom St Ina's is dedicated. A local tale tells of Ine, the Christian king of Wessex from AD688 to 726, being shipwrecked in the area. He was so well cared for by local people that he pledged to return. He kept his promise and, on returning, built a church here. A more likely claim is that the church is dedicated to St Ina, a fifth-century Welsh saint and member of Gwynedd's royal house.

Colourful coast: *Brightly painted, traditional fishing boats at New Quay*

After about 1 kilometre of beach walking, head up the substantial set of metal steps and gangway leading into the trees. Turn right along the clear path. Immediately after it bends sharp left, climb the steps on the right. The 'photo point' and picnic bench in a short while provide a great place to sit and admire the views across to the town and its bay. You soon join a gravel driveway that passes to the right of several cottages and then climbs to the **B4342**. Those who took the high-tide alternative rejoin the main route here.

10 Turn right and walk along the main road for about 150 metres. Head down the dead-end lane on the right — **Pilot Lane**. At the gate to **Seafields**, turn left along the surfaced walkway. Resisting the lure of the **beer garden** in a short while, you'll come out on to a quiet road close to the **Black Lion pub**. Turn right and head downhill, passing **New Quay's harbour beach** and an assortment of **pubs** and **cafés**. Just after the **public toilets**, follow the road round to the left and you'll soon see **The Corner Shop** and **Post Office** on your left. This is where today's section ends.

High-tide alternative:
From **Pont Llanina**, continue along the narrow road until you reach the **B4342**. Turn right to walk along the pavement towards New Quay,

rejoining the main route when it too comes up onto the main road (at waypoint 10 in the main route description above). This alternative route adds only 250 metres to today's total distance.

New Quay harbour is popular with visitors

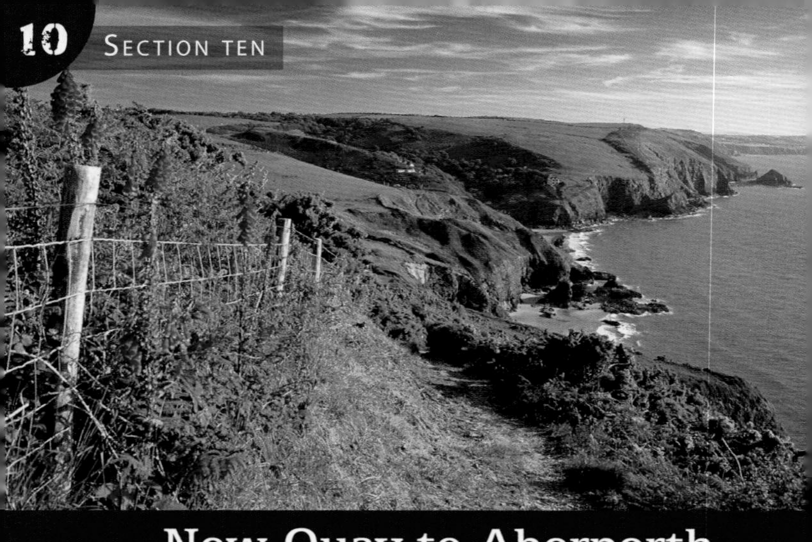

New Quay to Aberporth

Distance: *21 kilometres / 13 miles* | **Start:** *The Corner Shop and Post Office, South John Street, New Quay SH 389 600* | **Finish:** *Dolphin sculpture, Aberporth SN 258 515* | **Maps:** *Ordnance Survey Explorer 198 Cardigan and New Quay, Landranger 145 Cardigan and Mynydd Preseli*

Outline: Coastal walking at its best! A magnificent but tough day along windswept cliffs towering over secluded beaches and jagged stacks.

This is a strenuous day involving a lot of climbing, but the superb coastal scenery makes it well worth the effort. Some stretches feel quite remote, although several villages are passed along the way. The obvious place to cut section 10 short is Llangrannog, 13 kilometres (8.5 miles) into the day. The highlight is the dramatic, exposed cliff walk south of Cwmtydu, although vertigo sufferers might prefer to take the inland alternative. This adds 2 kilometres (1.2 miles) to the total distance.

Services: *The small resort of New Quay has a range of places to stay and eat, as well as shops, public toilets and cash machine. En-route, there is a seasonal café, public toilets and B&B accommodation at Cwmtydu; pubs, cafés, B&Bs and small shop at Llangrannog; café and public toilets at Penbryn; and a pub, B&Bs and public toilets at Tresaith. Aberporth has a slightly wider range of accommodation and places to eat as well as campsites, but little in the way of shops. A2 Taxis, Aberporth | 01239 814928 or 07795 802082 | www.aberporth-taxis.co.uk*

Don't miss: New Quay Marine Wildlife Centre – good displays | **Afon Soden** – rare butterflies | **Llangrannog** – pretty village and impressive coast

▲ *Cliffs beyond New Quay*

New Quay

Like many Welsh coastal settlements, New Quay's early life was based on fishing and shipbuilding. The first quay was built in the late seventeenth century by local fishermen, and shipbuilding began in the 1770s. The sea continues to play a major role in the town's economy: while shipbuilding ceased in 1878 and the fishing of lobsters, whelks and crabs continues on only a small scale, tourists flock to the town during the summer. Beach holidays, wildlife watching and off-shore fishing trips all contribute to a busy season.

No visitor to New Quay can fail to notice the town's oft-proclaimed links with the poet Dylan Thomas. He lived here for a while during the mid-1940s. The Wales Coast Path's high-tide route into New Quay (see Day Section nine) passes Majoda, where the writer, his wife Caitlin and their children lived from September 1944 until July 1945. Just "a shack at the edge of the cliff", with no running water or electricity, it cost them £1 a week to rent. He described it as a "wood and asbestos pagoda" where his children "hop like fleas in a box". Today, Majoda is a more substantial bungalow, but a mock-up of the original building was erected in a neighbouring field for the 2008 film, *The Edge of Love*, starring Matthew Rhys as Dylan Thomas.

Lobster pots on the shore at New Quay

The route: **New Quay to Aberporth**

1 With your back to **The Corner Shop** and **Post Office** in New Quay, turn left along **South John Street** and then, staying on the **seafront**, turn right along **Wellington Place**. Go through the kissing-gate at the road-end and, almost immediately, head steeply up the bare slope on the left. Swinging left, walk with an exposed cliff-face up to the right. Immediately after a surfaced turning area, climb the steps on your right. Turn right again on reaching a minor road, and then, at the last house, take the path to the right of the garden wall. This soon climbs steeply on to the **cliff-top**.

This is a fine and often exciting section of the Wales Coast Path. *As the path twists and turns, it allows walkers snatched glimpses of the contorted rocks on the cliffs. Both folding and faulting are apparent between New Quay and Aberporth.* When the path splits, take either option. The one to the left simply avoids an exposed section of cliff that may make for uncomfortable walking in strong winds. The two branches are quickly reunited just before you pass a lookout shelter above **Birds Rock**. The views ahead are very dramatic now, revealing some of the most impressive coastal scenery since leaving Porthmadog.

In the summer, Birds Rock is an important nesting site for seabirds. As many as 4,000 guillemots turn the rock into a seabird city from April to August — with the help of large numbers of kittiwakes as well as some fulmars, razorbills and shags. Chough and stonechat can also be seen along this stretch of coast. The cliff-top shelter here used to be a Coastguard look-out station, but it has since been renovated and is now used mostly for monitoring Cardigan Bay's significant population of bottlenose dolphins.

2 After a couple of gates, the route plunges valley-ward on a steep and often

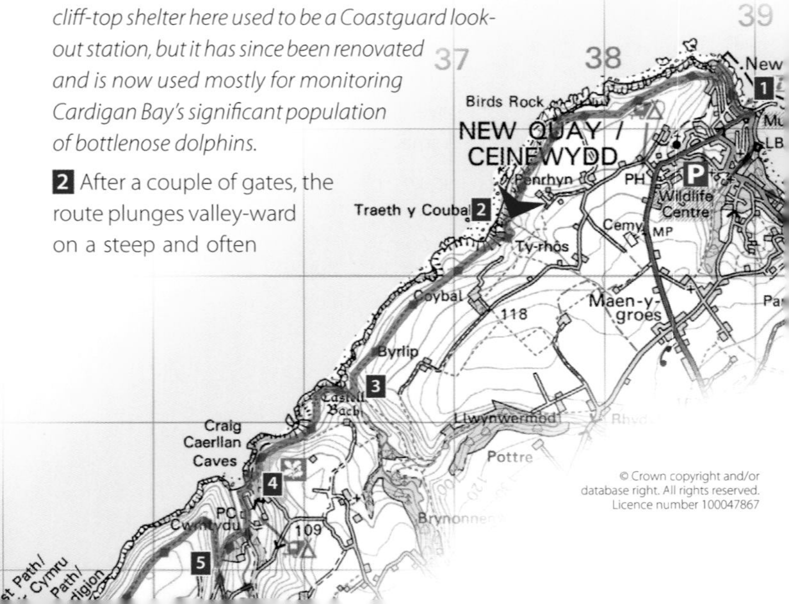

High and dry: *From New Quay, the path heads south around the cliffs*

loose path. Having climbed the steps on the other side of **Nant y Grogal**, keep right at a fork. After a gate, go through a gap in the hedgerow on your right and drop to a **gated bridge**. Once across this, the path climbs steadily. As it does so, take some time to look behind at the dramatic cliffs you've just negotiated.

After a kissing-gate, head down the steep slope on the right. The path then winds its way down to a bridge over the **Afon Soden** at **Cwm Silio**. Keep right at a fork on the way down. A small beach is accessible here at low tide.

The valley of the Afon Soden is known for its butterflies, including a number of relatively rare species. The common blue and wall brown can be spotted on the cliffs nearby. The latter gets its name from its habit of basking on bare surfaces, including walls, with its wings partly open. The sun's warmth hits the butterfly directly but is also reflected from the surface on which it is resting. Further up the valley, the National Trust regularly carries out work to ensure the survival of the pearl-bordered fritillary butterfly, a species that has been in rapid decline over the last few decades and is now found in only a few sites in Wales. Other butterfly and moth species that can be seen in this area include the dingy skipper, green hairstreak, speckled yellow, cinnabar, silver-washed fritillary and the rare white-spotted sable, a day-flying moth.

Sheltered cove: *Cwmtydu nestles in an enclosed valley*

3 Climbing out of the other side of **Cwm Silio**, you reach a fork beyond the first set of steps. Bear right here, ignoring the steps to the left. The path winds its way round the small headland near **Castell Bach** on close-cropped turf and then cuts across the next cliff.

Castell Bach is just one of many dozens of Iron Age promontory forts along the Ceredigion and Pembrokeshire coasts. Dating back to about 300BC, some of its ramparts are still clearly visible, although much of it has been lost to coastal erosion.

On the descent to **Cwmtydu**, keep right at a signposted fork. A sharp bend to the left then drops you close to the sea wall and a **lime kiln**.

The shales and grits that form the cliffs in this area were laid down in the Silurian period, about 400 million years ago. During the eighteenth century, caves that formed in the weaker rocks were used by smugglers. They would unload casks of brandy and bags of salt at low tide and store them in the caves until land-based distributors came to take them away — usually under cover of darkness.

4 Turn left along the road, soon passing a **café**. There are some **public toilets** set back from the road on your right in a short while: the coast path leaves the road here to pass to the left of the toilet block and cross a **bridge over the stream**. It heads uphill, soon swinging left to climb the wooded valley side.

5 After a kissing-gate, a path junction is reached. You now have a decision to make. The main coast path heads right. This is probably the most dramatic and exciting section between Porthmadog and Cardigan, but the trail cuts across high, steep-sided cliffs with vertiginous drops to the sea below. Although the path is fairly wide, some people may find the route unnerving in strong winds.

Inland alternative:

From waypoint **5** in the above walk description, to avoid the cliff path, turn left and drop to a quiet road at **Pen y parc**. Now turn right. It's a long, slow uphill plod, but, as the road gains height, it provides superb

The dramatic cliff path beyond Cwmtydu

Island in the stream: *On the coast path above Ynys Lochtyn*

views over the surrounding wooded valleys and dells, particularly in the autumn when the leaves have taken on a variety of hues.

A. After 550 metres of road walking, drop down the rough forestry track on the left. Soon after another track joins from the left, bear right at a fork. After crossing a small stream, bear right at another two forks. With bracken and brambles encroaching on the path in places, make your way to a stile. Having climbed this, go through the gate opposite and follow the path to the road.

B. Turn left. Take the next road on the right — signposted Llangrannog — and then turn left.

About 370 metres along this road, just as it begins to descend, take the signposted path on the right. Entering a narrow field, cross to the trees opposite and then head right to find a hidden stile. A trail leads through the trees to a track, along which you turn left. Pick up the continuation of the path by dropping down the steps in front of a cottage. After a small gate out of the woods, drop to a hedgerow and bear right to walk with it on your left. The next kissing-gate leads back into the trees.

C. On reaching a road — the **B4321** — take a few paces to the right and then step up on to a lovely woodland path running above the road. Go straight over at a crossing of paths. Turn right when you reach a minor road and then, almost immediately go through a metal gate on the left. Keeping close to the fence/hedgerow on your left, cross the next two fields and then turn right along a rough track.

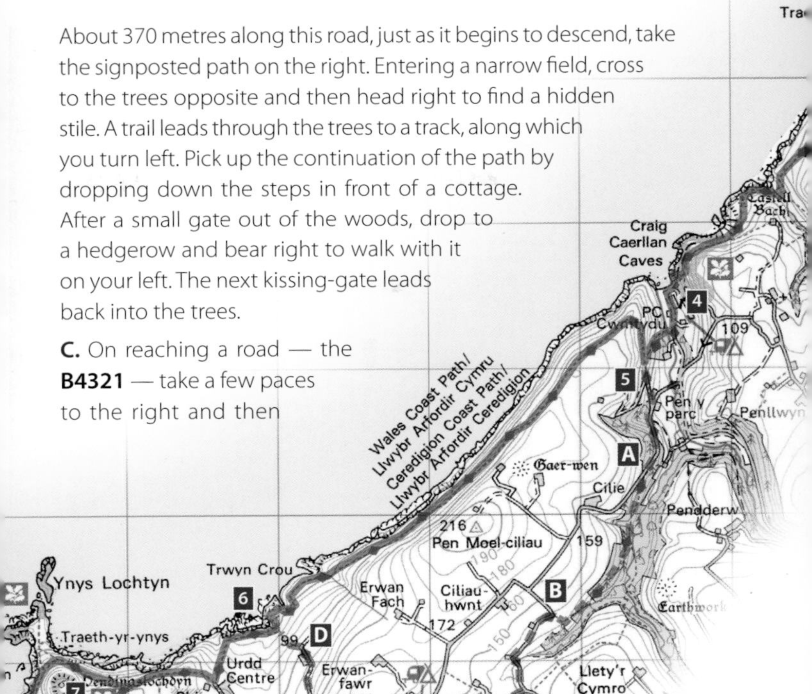

D. After 500 metres, the track bends sharp right. When it does so, go through the kissing-gate and head straight down the grassy slope towards a waymarker post. Continuing in the same direction, you'll reach a kissing-gate. Once through this, turn left and you're back on

Coastal charm: *The pretty seaside village of Llangrannog*

the main route again, picking it up at waypoint **6** in the main walk description above. This alternative route adds two kilometres to today's total distance.

Those who choose the sea-cliff route should turn right at Waypoint **5** quickly heading through a kissing-gate beside a larger gate. Having climbed for a while, there are grand views back of the section of coast just walked. The path crosses an old, grassed-over wall and then swings left, passing to the right of a slightly more substantial old wall. You're now back out on the cliff-top proper: a wonderful section of path with ponies grazing on the other side of the low wall. The excellently engineered path later drops slightly as it cuts across the cliff-face in spectacular fashion. The drops to the right are steep, but not sheer, and the ledge that the path follows is generally at least a couple of metres wide, so, unless you are genuinely scared of heights or a gale is blowing, the next few kilometres are a wonderful experience.

Sadly though, the original path, which can be seen cutting invitingly across the slope ahead, was made impassable by a landslide a few years ago. Soon after a gate, walkers are directed up the new, stonier path, rising to the left. The engineered track later zig-zags down from the high cliffs and continues

over the top of lower, grass-topped cliffs. *If you fancy an airy picnic spot where you can feel the briny breeze in your hair, the small headland of* **Trwyn Crou**, *possibly the site of another promontory fort, is just off route here.*

The path, now little more than a grassy trail, doesn't stick religiously to the cliff edge; it cuts the corner, eventually heading in the general direction of the **Urdd centre** on the hillside ahead. After a kissing-gate, you find yourself closer to the churning sea below.

St Carannog

Born at the end of the fifth century, St Carannog was the son of a South Wales ruler. His father wanted him to succeed him to the throne, but Carannog wished to spread the word of Jesus. He lived for a while as a hermit in a Llangrannog cave, and carried out missionary work in Ireland and southwest England. The saint's statue overlooking the village was sculpted by Sebastien Boyesen.

Summer scene: *Two walkers pause to look back at Llangrannog*

6 About 200 metres beyond the kissing-gate, you'll see another gate on the left. This is where the inland alternative, described later, rejoins the main coast path.

With a few stacks and rocky outcrops just offshore, the coast path winds its way across the cliff-tops. Having passed through a couple of gates, follow the fence uphill to the left. *A plaque beside the path commemorates the official opening of the Ceredigion Coast Path on July 3, 2008. It features verse by local poet and former National Eisteddfod archdruid Dic Jones, who sadly died the following year.* Nearing the buildings at the bottom of the **Urdd centre**'s dry ski slope, swing right.

The Urdd is Wales's largest youth movement, encouraging the personal and social development of young people through the Welsh medium. It was set up in 1922 by Sir Ifan ab Owen Edwards who wanted to save the language from what looked, at the time, like a bleak future. The Urdd now has four residential centres in Wales, including this one near Llangrannog, where youngsters have access to a range of facilities including stables, a climbing centre, swimming pool, quad bikes, go-karts and ski lessons.

Once you're up and over this hill, keep to the right of the fence. You'll soon see the ancient hill fort of **Pen y Badell** up ahead. *This was occupied between about 500BC and 500AD, and some flint tools were unearthed here.*

7 On reaching a gate close to the base of the prominent hill on which the fort is built, strike off right to contour its steep eastern and northern flanks. Keep left at a fork — unless you want to head out on to the exposed headland leading out towards **Ynys Lochtyn**. Having turned your back on the headland, watch for a small gate on the right. This provides access to a path that descends towards **Llangrannog**.

The complex collection of jagged coastal features to the southwest of the village is visible from here. The rocks in this area are largely Silurian and Ordovician, formed about 400 million years ago. The impressive sea stack of **Carreg Bica** *is one of the best known local landmarks. It is said to be the tooth of a giant, or possibly even the Devil himself, who spat it into the bay after suffering toothache. Sitting between Traeth Cilborth and the beach at Llangrannog, it can be visited at low tide. Indeed, if time and tides allow, this is a great section of the beach to explore — home to rock pools, smugglers' caves and dramatic cliffs.*

As you descend, you might spot an easy-to-miss path off to the right that leads down to the tidal beach at **Cilborth**. The steps here were cut into the cliffs in the 1920s. Unless you're going to visit the beach, continue on the main path. This drops to the little village of **Llangrannog**, possibly the most charming of Ceredigion's seaside settlements.

The sheltered beach and village at Tresaith

Cliff cascade: *Tresaith's spectacular waterfall plunges over the cliff into the sea*

Interpretation panels provide information on the village, putting the existing buildings into historic context. The flat area now occupied by the Ship Inn's car park, for example, was once home to a couple of lime kilns and was also used for building small ships. Tree trunks for shipbuilding were brought by cart from a local estate and then sawn into planks in a saw-pit above what is now the Patio Café.

8 Join the road that passes behind the beach and then winds its way up the hill on the other side of the tiny bay. Rejoin the cliff path behind the **statue of St Carannog**, which is just to the right of the road on a sharp left-hand bend.

As you make your way along the cliff path, turn round for a good view of Pen y Badell and a clear sighting of the vein of shiny, white quartz running through Ynys-Lochtyn.

After dropping steeply to cross a **wooden footbridge** over a small stream, bear right when the path splits. Beyond a gate, head half-left up the grassy slope, initially aiming to the right of a mast. You never actually reach the mast though; instead, the path swings off to the right. When the cliff path ends, you find yourself on a broad track heading gently downhill. Go through a large metal gate to the right of some **farm buildings** and then turn left along a minor road.

9 There are **public toilets** and a **café** here at **Penbryn**, but you head off to the right, across the car park, just before reaching them. A path now heads into the gorgeous, dark woodland. After crossing a **bridge**, turn right at a path junction near the top of the steps. Keep left along the higher route when the path splits, but then ignore a path off to the left — leading to the church — in a short while. As you leave the trees and step back out into the open, you can see the long, inviting **Traeth Penbryn** below. (There's a set of steps on your right in a short while should you fancy a paddle.)

James Bond fans may feel a sense of déjà vu on seeing Traeth Penbryn. That's because the beach featured in the 2002 Bond film Die Another Day *with Pierce Brosnan in the starring role and Penbryn doing its best impersonation of North Korea.*

The climb between Penbryn and Tresaith seems endless, particularly for those who have walked all the way from New Quay. It reaches a high point of about 140 metres just below a look-out post. But, as you'll be all too aware by now, what goes up must come down, and you'll barely have had time to appreciate the long-distance views before the path starts descending to **Tresaith**.

10 Turn right on reaching a road and, in about 30 metres, head down the steps to the right of the **bus shelter**. At the bottom of the steps, you're close to all of **Tresaith's** sparse but welcome facilities: a **pub**, **public toilets** and a seasonal **beach shop**. *At low tide, it's worth heading down to the beach to have a look at the* **spectacular waterfall** *formed by* **Afon Saith** *as it plummets over the exposed cliff-face. It's reached by bearing right along the sand.* Continuing along the Wales Coast Path, turn left along the road and then drop down the slipway. You'll soon find a path, at the back of the beach, rising back onto the cliffs.

The cliffs between Tresaith and **Aberporth** are nowhere near as high or as undulating as what's gone before. Indeed, the final section is on a surfaced mobility path suitable for motorised scooters. On the edge of Aberporth, follow this round to the left and then the right. Head straight down the lane between some houses and then turn right at a T-junction (close to some public toilets). When the road ends, you'll pick up an obvious path. This soon swings left. Keep left at a fork — along the wider of the two routes — and then go right at a second fork, close to an information panel. Turn right at the road, soon passing the **Ship Inn** on your left. As the road swings left, watch for a **sculpture of a dolphin** to the right: this is where today's section ends.

Aberporth to Cardigan

Distance: *21 kilometres / 13 miles* | **Start:** *Dolphin sculpture, Aberporth SN 258 515* | **Finish:** *Otter sculpture beside Afon Teifi, Cardigan SN 177 458* | **Maps:** *Ordnance Survey Explorer 198 Cardigan and New Quay, Landranger 145 Cardigan and Mynydd Preseli*

Outline: Steep-sided cwms, picturesque cliffs and tiny coves that are home to tempting beaches are typical of the final day's walking.

Another beautiful, rugged section of Welsh coast is encountered between the attractive settlements of Aberporth and Cardigan. The gradients aren't as brutal as on previous days though, so the walking is easier — more chance to enjoy the spectacular surroundings and watch for wildlife. As you make your way along cliffs carpeted in wildflowers, the highlights include the gorgeous beach and chapel at Mwnt. The final few kilometres are completed on minor roads and farmland along the eastern shore of the Teifi estuary.

Services: *Aberporth has a range of accommodation and places to eat as well as campsites, but little in the way of shops. Cardigan has a much better choice of facilities, including accommodation, nearby campsite, places to eat, cash machines and shops. However, there are very few facilities en-route other than a campsite, public toilets and seasonal kiosk selling drinks and snacks at Mwnt; and a hotel with restaurant at Gwbert near the end of the day. Robins Taxis, Cardigan | 01239 612190*

Don't miss: **Mwnt Church** – medieval chapel of ease for sailors | **Cardigan** – colourful market town | **St Dogmaels** – picturesque twelfth-century ruins just over county border in Pembrokeshire

▲ *Mwnt Church at sunset*

Aberporth

Aberporth was named as a satellite of the port of Cardigan in the sixteenth century and, by 1700, was welcoming a large number of trading vessels. By the middle of the nineteenth century, when the village was home to a number of ship-owning families, its main imports were limestone, coal and slate. During winter though, when the trading vessels were laid up, local people turned their hand to fishing — and Aberporth became one of main centres of the herring trade in Wales.

The crew of a herring smack would usually consist of about six men. The boats, up to seven metres long, tended to have two masts, although the crew might have to use long oars in relatively calm conditions. The smacks would often operate in pairs, with nets secured between the two boats as they drifted between Mwnt and Llangrannog. Alternatively, the nets would be set with weights holding them in place.

The herring industry died out about 100 years ago. Lobster and crab fishing continue today, but the two biggest employers in the village in the twenty-first century are the tourist industry and the military testing site, run by a private company on behalf of the Ministry of Defence (MoD).

The sandy beach at Aberporth

The route: Aberporth to Cardigan

1 From the **dolphin sculpture** in **Aberporth**, take the lane heading northwest. (There's a small car park on the right here.) After passing above a lovely beach, the road climbs steeply, eventually entering **Parcllyn**. You'll soon walk beside the barbed wire-topped fence of the **MoD's Aberporth site**. Go right at a T-junction close to the entrance to the base and then take the next turning on the right.

The MoD's Aberporth base is the reason why the coast path has to make another inland detour. The 220-hectare site controls a testing range that covers 6,500 square kilometres of Cardigan Bay. There's been a military range here since World War Two, and today it's used for testing air-launched weapons and drones.

2 Just before the double gates leading into the MoD property, go through a kissing-gate on the left. Walk with the hedgerow on your left and then, after the next gate, walk diagonally across the field. A white-topped post acts as a guide. In the far corner of the field, beyond two gates in quick succession, you enter an area of dense vegetation. Quickly reaching a path junction, turn right. Just after a gate leads back out into the open, go straight across at a grassy track. The path eventually follows the southern rim of the **Allt y Gwrddon** back out to the sea. Veering west, you'll be able to see the cliffs stretching out ahead of you again. Soon after crossing the first of several **wooden footbridges**, watch for a cave in the cliffs below, close to the tiny tidal beach of **Traeth Gwrddon**.

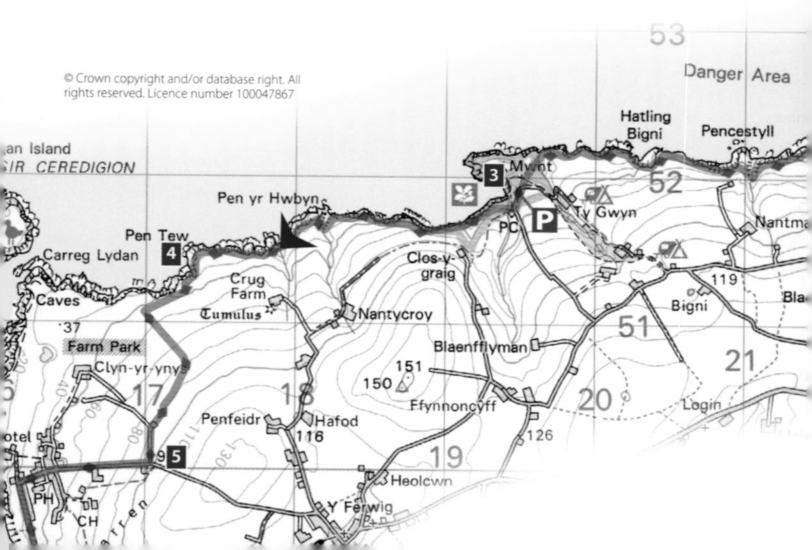

Purple haze: *Foxgloves colour the cliff path in early summer*

This part of the coast path is fairly straightforward. As on the previous section, streams have cut many steep-sided ravines into this stretch of the cliff; unlike the previous section, however, there isn't a huge amount of descent and ascent involved in crossing them.

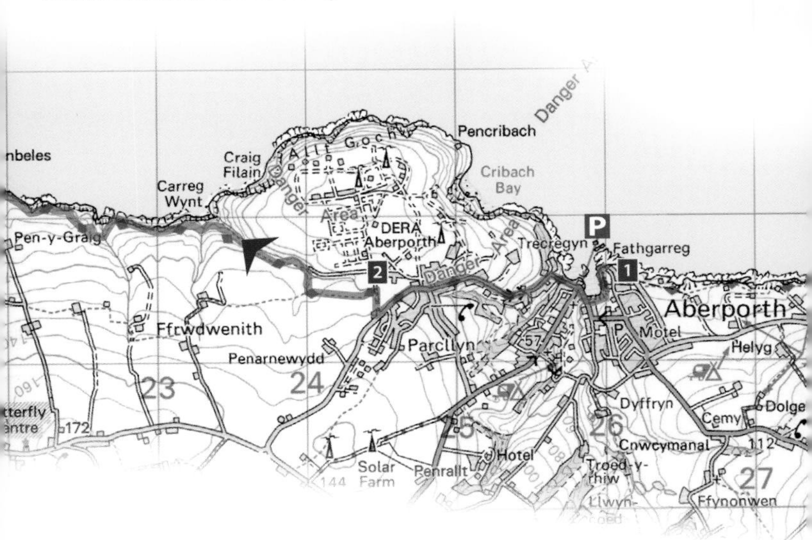

Iconic spot: *Mwnt Church and beach are tucked below the conical hill of Foel-y-Mwnt*

The rocks of **Pen-Peles** jut out into the sea about 1.6km west of Traeth Gwrddon. Just beyond them, the path drops to cross another **footbridge**. Immediately after this, keep right as a path goes left to **Llwyn-ysgaw**. Soon after passing some more militaristic-looking contraptions up on the hillside — and signs warning of 'non-ionizing radiation' — you'll see a conical hill ahead. This is **Foel-y-Mwnt**, a well-known and much photographed local landmark.

Nearing the base of Foel-y-Mwnt, go through a gate and head up to the left, beside a fence. After crossing a small **stream**, don't be tempted by a couple of lesser trails to the left; simply keep straight on, passing to the left of the simple, white-washed **church of the Holy Cross**.

On sunny summer weekends, Mwnt is a popular spot for locals and tourists alike. Catch it at a quiet time though, and it's a very tranquil spot. The tiny church — watch your head on the low door on the way in! — was restored after storm damage in 1917. It contains an early font, possibly twelfth century, made from stone from Pembrokeshire's Preseli Hills.

In 1155, Fleming invaders landed on the sheltered beach at Mwnt. The bloody

skirmish that followed is commemorated on the first Sunday of January as Sul Coch y Mwnt, or Mwnt Red Sunday.

3 Turn right when you reach a minor road close to the Mwnt car park. After about 170 metres, drop to the **public toilets** and **seasonal kiosk**. Pass above the **lime kiln**, and, of the two continuing paths, take the one on the right, soon passing through a kissing-gate. As you begin to climb, keep to the main path. You'll soon have a good view back to Foel-y-Mwnt.

Mwnt church

The wonderfully situated, white-washed church at Mwnt was probably built in the fourteenth century, although there had been a holy site here for centuries before that. It may have been a place of vigil for saints' bodies on their way to their traditional Bardsey Island burial ground. Later, in medieval times, it served as a chapel of ease for sailors who couldn't easily reach the nearest parish church.

The next couple of kilometres consist of some spectacular coastal scenery. The cliffs may not be particularly high, but they are truly dramatic, especially when rough seas are battering the rocks below. The island soon visible ahead is **Cardigan Island**.

During a massive storm in 1934, a 7,000-tonne liner ran aground on Cardigan Island, changing the face of this small land mass forever. The SS Herefordshire was being towed from Dartmouth in Devon to a breakers' yard on the Clyde when the tow ropes broke. She came to rest on Cardigan Island. The four tugmen aboard managed to scramble ashore, but they weren't the only ones to set foot on the island: a number of brown rats also abandoned the sinking ship. Before they were finally eradicated more than 30 years later, they caused a tremendous amount of soil erosion and totally wiped out the island's puffin colony. Sadly, despite attempts by the Wildlife Trust of South and West Wales to lure them back by placing wooden decoy puffins on the cliffs, the birds have never returned. But there are other species breeding on the uninhabited island, including razorbill, guillemot, shag, fulmar, chough and various types of gull. Grey seals also breed in the sea caves.

4 Having skirted the edge of a few fields, you'll see a tiny, quarried rock face to the left. The path heads inland soon after this. At the far side of this field, turn left to walk with the field boundary on your right. In the top corner, turn right — through a pair of gates — and

Striding out: *On the cliff path west of Mwnt with Cardigan Island ahead*

then turn left. Keeping to the edge of the field, follow the field boundary round to the right in a short while. Beyond the next gate, continue with the field boundary on your left for about 80 metres and then watch for two gates on the left. They're not easy to spot until you're standing next to them. Once through them, keep close to the field boundary on the right and follow it all the way to the road.

5 Turn right along the road. With Pembrokeshire soon in sight on the other side of the mouth of the **Afon Teifi**, you reach the **Gwbert Hotel** in **Gwbert**. Follow the road, known as **Coronation Drive**, round to the left. There is a surfaced walkway to the right of the asphalt. The road route continues for another 2 kilometres, past the **holiday park** and **Teifi Boating Club**.

The salt marsh beside the Afon Teifi is home to marsh samphire and sea aster. Further north, orchids and evening primroses bring a splash of colour to the dunes in the summer. In you're here during the autumn, watch for waders such as curlew, redshank and oystercatchers feeding on the mudflats.

6 Only after the road swings away from the estuary, do you embark on another cross-country route. Just past a couple of buildings, take the broad track on the right — signposted Cardigan. Swing left to pass to the right of the **Swallow Boats**' sheds, where luxury yachts are built, and then carry straight

River town: *Cardigan seen across the Afon Teifi*

on to a small metal gate. Once through this, walk beside the field boundary on your right and then cross a wooden step stile. The path continues to the right of a fence, swings left and goes through a gap to enter a small field, which sometimes has maize growing in it. Go straight across the field at first and then swing up to the left to pass through a small kissing-gate. The path negotiates a couple of fields and then comes out on to a surfaced lane near **Bryn-y-mor House**.

Cross over and go through the metal kissing-gate. Turn right to walk along the field edge, following it round two left-hand bends. Shortly after the second bend, drop right to enter a wooded dell via a gate. On the other side of this, turn right as you enter the next field. Go through the small gate just in from the field corner and then turn sharp left. The village on the other side of the water is St Dogmaels, the official starting point of the Pembrokeshire Coast Path — 300 kilometres of some of the best coastal walking in the whole of the British Isles. Leaving the field, continue along a broad track between the hedgerows until it emerges on a quiet lane along which you turn right.

7 Walk along the asphalt for about 300 metres, and then turn left through a kissing-gate. On the other side of this large field, turn left along a clear, shady path just up from the water's edge. Beyond a **sewage treatment**

works, join a surfaced lane. Soon after passing a slipway, step on to the path heading right. Keep close to the water and then, when you drop to the river's edge, turn left to pass a boat that doubles up as an **Indian restaurant**.

Veer right and cross the lower part of the **car park**. Past some buildings, head up the one-way street rising slightly right. At the main road, turn right to drop to the **two bridges** over the **Afon Teifi** — an old road bridge and a newer footbridge. An **otter sculpture** marks the conclusion of the **Ceredigion Coast Path**. Over the other side of the river, the gorgeous Pembrokeshire Coast Path awaits......

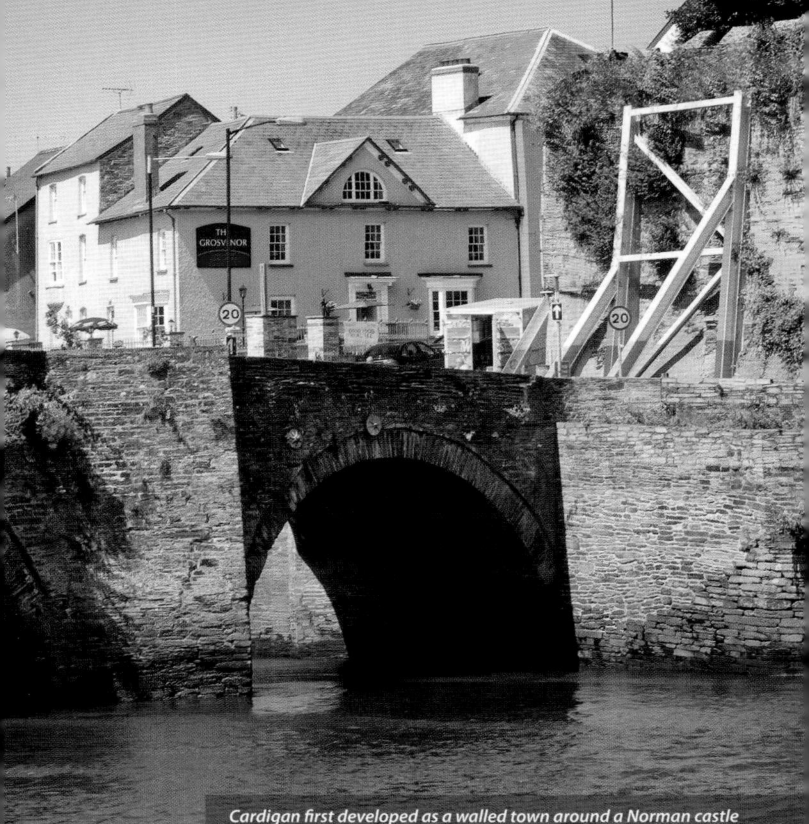

Cardigan first developed as a walled town around a Norman castle

"Wales, where the past still lives. Where every place has its tradition, every name its poetry ..."

Matthew Arnold, *On the Study of Celtic Literature*, 1866

Welsh coastal place names

Welsh place names are as much a part of Wales's cultural distinctiveness as its mountains, sheep or rugged coast. To the English visitor, they may appear strangely foreign, confusing or simply unpronounceable. And yet, once carefully unravelled, they can tell us all sorts of fascinating things about a place — its landscape, character and history. Even these few common place name elements should help bring the Wales Coast Path alive.

Welsh	Meaning	Pronunciation
Aber	river mouth, estuary	*Ab-er*
Afon	river	*Av-on*
Bad	ferry, boat	*Bad*
Bae	bay	*Bai*
Cae	field, enclosure	*Kai*
Carreg	stone, rock	*Kar-reg*
Cawl	sea kale	*Kowl*
Cei	quay	*Kay*
Cilfach	cove, creek	*Kil-vakh*
Clegyr	rock, cliff	Kleg-ir
Culfor	strait	*Kil-vor*
Din/dinas	citadel; hillfort; fortified hill	*Deen/Deen-as*
Dŵr/dwfr	water	*Doer/Doo-vr*
Dyffryn	valley; bottom	*Duff-ryn*
Eglwys	church	*Eg-looees*
Ffynnon	well; spring; fountain; source	*Fun-on*

Goleudy	lighthouse	*Gol-ay-dee*
Glan	shore	*Glan*
Gwymon	seaweed	*Gwi-mon*
Harbwr	harbour	*Haboor*
Heli	salt water, brine	*Hel-lee*
Llech	flat stone, flagstone, slate	*Th-lekh*
Maen	stone; standing stone	*Mine*
Môr	sea, ocean	*More*
Morfa	sea marsh, salt marsh	*Mor-va*
Moryd	estuary, channel	*Mor-rid*
Ogof	cave	*Og-ov*
Parrog	flat land by the sea	*Par-rog*
Penrhyn	headland	*Pen-rin*
Pigyn	point	*Pig-in*
Pont/bont	bridge, arch	*Pont/Bont*
Porth	harbour	*Porth*
Pwll	pool, pit	*Pooth*
Tafol	dock	*Tav-ol*
Ton/don	wave	*Ton/Don*
Traeth	beach	*Treye-th*
Trwyn	nose; point, cape	*Troo-een*
Tywyn	sandy shore sand dunes	*Tow-in*
Ynys	island	*Un-iss*

Useful Information

Wales Coast Path

Comprehensive information about all sections of the Wales Coast Path can be found on the official website at **www.walescoastpath.gov.uk**, **www.walescoastpath.co.uk** and **www.ceredigioncoastpath.org.uk**

'Visit Wales'

The Visit Wales website covers everything from accommodation to attractions. For information on the areas covered by this book, see **www.visitwales.com/explore/north-wales/snowdonia-mountains-coast** for the Snowdonia section and **www.visitwales.com/explore/mid-wales/ceredigion** for Ceredigion.

Snowdonia and Ceredigion

For local information, from what to do to eating out, see **www.visitsnowdonia**.info or w**ww.discoverceredigion.wales**

Tourist Information Centres

The Tourist Information Centres provide free information on everything from accommodation and travel to what's on and walking advice.

Aberdyfi	01654 767321	tic.aberdyfi@eryri-npa.org.uk
Aberystwyth	01970 612125	aberystwythtic@ceredigion.gov.uk
Beddgelert	01766 890615	tic.beddgelert@eryri-npa.gov.uk

Where to stay

There's lots of accommodation close to the Snowdonia and Ceredigion Coast section of the Wales Coast Path, from campsites, youth hostels and B&Bs to holiday cottages and hotels. Tourist Information Centre staff will know what's available locally and can even book for you. Alternatively, book online. Find campsites at **www.ukcampsite.co.uk**

Luggage-carrying service

For door-to-door luggage transfer between overnight stops in Ceredigion, try Walkalongway, 01834 869997 or 07976 926165 | **www.walkalongway.com**

Walking holidays

Several companies offer complete walking packages including accommodation, local information, maps, luggage transfer and transport.

Celtic Trails | 01291 689774 | **www.celtic-trails.com** | info@celtic-trails.com

Contours | 01629 821900 | **www.contours.co.uk** | info@contours.co.uk

Dragon Trails | 07850 174875 | **www.dragontrails.com** | richard@dragontrails.com

Edge of Wales Walk | 01758 760652 | **www.edgeofwaleswalk.co.uk** | enquiries@edgeofwaleswalk.co.uk

Encounter Walking | 01208 871066 | **www.encounterwalkingholidays.com** info@encounterwalkingholidays.com

Wales Walking Holidays | 01248 713611 | **www.waleswalkingholidays.com**

Trains and buses

For public transport information across Wales, see Traveline Cymru, 0871 200 22 33, **www.traveline-cymru.info**

The beginning and end of all the day sections from Porthmadog to Aberystwyth are on regular train services. For the first four days, there are stations every few miles as the coast path and the railway line run almost parallel with each other. All rail services in Wales are run by Arriva Trains Wales. For more information on timetables and fares, visit **www.arrivatrainswales.co.uk** or National Rail Enquiries, **www.nationalrail.co.uk**.

South of Aberystwyth, walkers are best served by local buses. Visit **www.discoverceredigion.wales** for details of the Cardi Bach bus between New Quay and Cardigan, or **www.ceredigion.gov.uk** for information on other routes.

Taxis

Porthmadog: Ralio Rownd | 07950 176551

Barmouth: Blue Line Cabs | 07585 855243

Aberdyfi: Dyfi Cabs | 07831 551538

Machynlleth: Peter's Taxi | 07969 997039

Aberystwyth: Cymru Cabs | 07951 580227

Aberporth: A2 Taxis | 01239 814928 or 07795 802082

Cardigan: Robins Taxi | 01239 612190

Cycle hire

Bike bike bike bike, 29-30 Pendre, Cardigan, SA43 1LA | 01239 621275

www.bikebikebike.co.uk | shop@bikebikebike.bike

Birmingham Garage, Church Street, Barmouth, LL42 1EL | 01341 280644 **www.birminghamgaragebikehire.com**

Cycle repairs

Summit Cycles, 65 North Parade, Aberystwyth, Ceredigion, SY23 2JN | 01970 626061 | **www.summitcycles.co.uk**

Emergencies

In an emergency, call 999 or 112 and ask for the service you require: ambulance, police, fire or coastguard.

Tides

Some beach sections of the Snowdonia and Ceredigion section of the Wales Coast Path can only be walked at low tide. To avoid difficulties, check tide times before you go. Tide table booklets are available from TICs and local shops. Tide tables for several locations between Porthmadog and Cardigan can also be viewed online at **www.tidetimes.org.uk**

Weather forecasts

For reliable and up-to-date weather forecasts, see **www.bbc.co.uk/weather** or **www.metoffice.gov.uk**

Annual events

Cardigan River and Food Festival: celebrating local independent food producers; early August | **www.cardigan-food-festival.co.uk**

Machynlleth Comedy Festival: weekend of stand-up comedy every spring | **www.machcomedyfest.co.uk**

Machynlleth Festival: cultural event, largely music, every August | **www.moma.machynlleth.org.u**k

MusicFest: A week of performance, courses and workshops in Aberystwyth every summer | **www.musicfestaberystwyth.org**.

Wales Coast Path: Official Guides

The **Official Guides** to the **Wales Coast Path** are endorsed by Natural Resources Wales, the Welsh government body which developed and manage the path. The guides break the Wales Coast Path into seven main sections, giving long-distance and local walkers everything they need to enjoy all 870 miles of this world-class route.

North Wales Coast
Chester to Bangor
ISBN: 978-1-914589-00-3

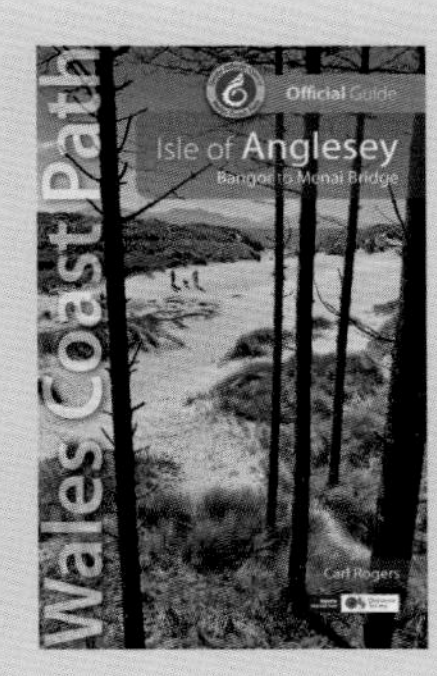

Isle of Anglesey
Circuit from Menai Bridge
ISBN: 978-1-914589-01-0

Llŷn Peninsula
Bangor to Porthmadog
ISBN: 978-1-914589-02-7

Pembrokeshire
Cardigan to Amroth
ISBN: 978-1-908632-98-2

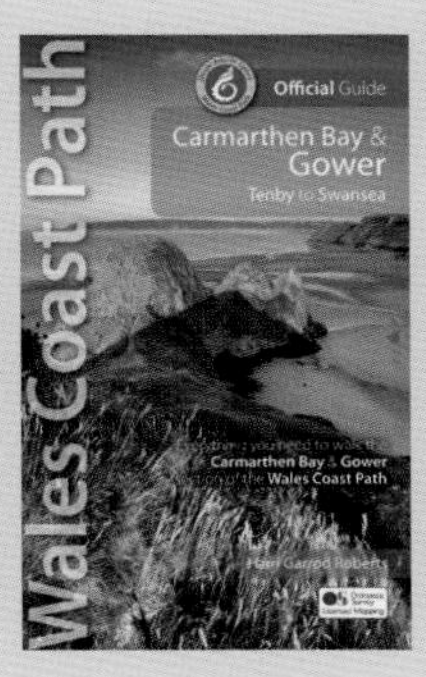

Carmarthenshire & Gower
Tenby to Swansea
ISBN: 978-1-908632-99-9

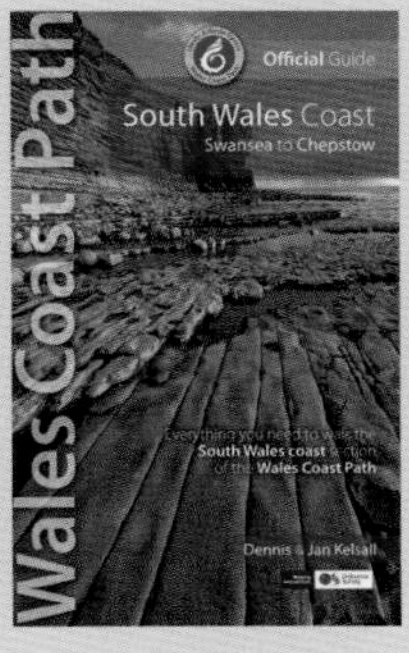

South Wales Coast
Swansea to Chepstow
ISBN: 978-1-914589-04-1

Wales Coast Path: Top 10 Walks

Award-winning pocket-size walking guides to the most popular, easy circular walks along key sections of the Wales Coast Path. The full series will cover the whole path in ten attractive guides.

Currently available

Top 10 Walks:
Llŷn Peninsula
ISBN: 978-1-902512-34-1

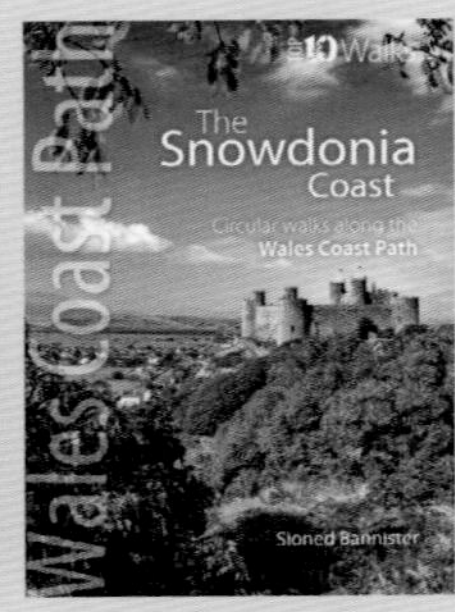

Top 10 Walks:
Snowdonia Coast
ISBN: 978-1 908632-85-2

Top 10 Walks:
Ceredigion Coast
ISBN: 978-1 908632-28-9

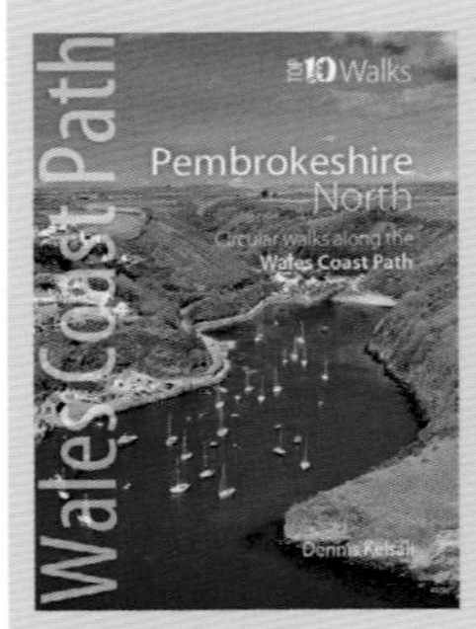

Top 10 Walks:
Pembrokeshire North
ISBN: 978-1-908632-29-6

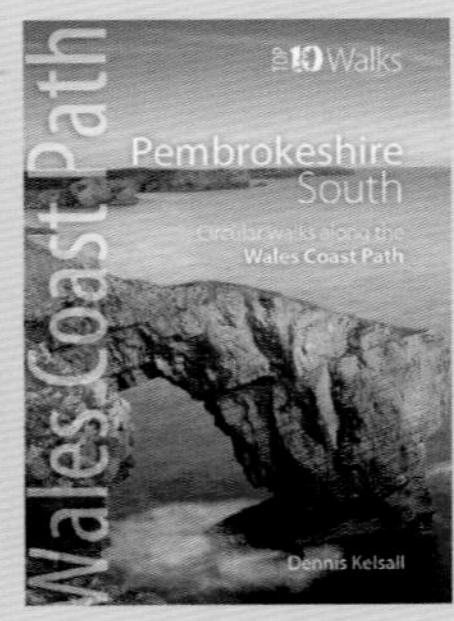

Top 10 Walks:
Pembrokeshire South
ISBN: 978-1-908632-30-2

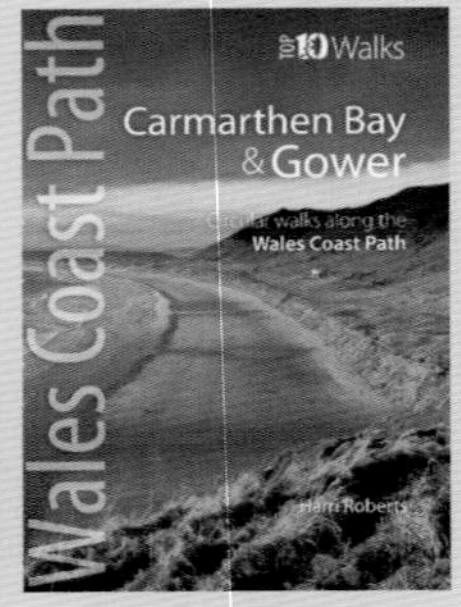

Top 10 Walks:
Carmarthenshire & Gower
ISBN: 978-1-908632-16-6